HANNAH

AND

THE

MASTER

I SPOKE OF *"BEAUTY."*

WHO MAY REACH

INTO THE *DEPTHS OF TERROR*

BUT LOVERS?

HANNAH

AND

THE

MASTER

JOSHUA COREY

MadHat Press
MadHat Incorporated
PO Box 422, Cheshire MA 01225

Copyright © 2021 Joshua Corey
All rights reserved

The Library of Congress has assigned
this edition a Control Number of
2020951620

ISBN 978-1-952335-15-0 (paperback)

Text by Joshua Corey
Cover design by F. J. Bergmann
Book design by Janet Holmes
Cover image: Anselm Kiefer, *Winter Landscape*. ©2014. Image copyright
The Metropolitan Museum of Art/Art Resource/Scala, Florence / © Anselm Kiefer
Photo of Hannah Arendt courtesy of the Granger Historical Picture Archive

www.MadHat-Press.com

CONTENTS

PROLOGUE : THE CENTURY // 5

CLOCKWISE / THE WAVE // 7

THE SHIELDS / LOVE SONGS OF HANNAH R. // 25

COUNTERCLOCKWISE \ VOIGT-KAMPFF // 57

HANNAHLEIDER / RED THREAD // 71

COUNTERCLOCKWISE \ SAINT WORLD // 95

GAIAGONY / HANNAH FURIOSA // 117

NOTES // 157

ACKNOWLEDGMENTS // 177

We live under dark skies and—there are few human beings.
—PAUL CELAN

. . . thinking and writing are (like the theater) . . .
—MARIE LUISE KNOTT

Why not invent a new kind of play—as for instance
Woman thinks: . . .
He does.
Organ Plays.
She writes.
They say:
She sings:
Night speaks:
They miss

—VIRGINIA WOOLF

We hate the people who try to make us form the connections we do not want to form.
—SIMONE WEIL

Forgiveness is the only way to reverse the irreversible flow of history.
—HANNAH ARENDT

AUCTORES LUDENS
(in order of appearance)

THE WAVE.

THE MASTER. A thinker from Germany. Alias MARTIN R.

THE POET. Joint author of the century's suicide note.

HANNAH. Jew, writer, thinker, lover. Alias DAISY, alias R., alias HANNAH R., alias HANNAH FURIOSA.

BEING.

THE PLAGIARIST. An author.

THE CALIBRATOR. Man unthinking.

THE DOCTOR. More human than human.

JOSHUA. A general.

SAINT WORLD.

Assorted TITANS, REPLICANTS, and ATTENDANTS.

THE CENTURY

A simple, perilous question: what forms does silence take in the world of today?

As usual: the silence of the poor and the exploited, of seas and animals and the earth's crust, the silence of the silenced.

But also: silence of the mind in slow evolved connection with other minds. Silence of reading, silence of thought.

Thoughts unthinkable of a life outside the structures of consumption and possession, sheer incapacities of the normal mind.

Thoughts of the "away" in distance and time where our goods are manufactured and our pollution is thrown. Thoughts of the future. Thoughts of a history without victors.

In the camps the spark of life sinks below the brightness of an ember. In the rafts of migrants, in heat islands, in urban centers dissected by war. Merely moving bodies tossed ghostly on the pile. Yet "life" "goes on." Doesn't it?

Climatology means "logic of the zone." *Climate* has its origins in the Greek *klinein*, to slope. Climate operates by inclination in the ashen light.

Silence of the winter sun, the summer sun. Silence ripening. Austere silence of the world passing away, in flood.

Not a WAVE out of Hokusai but "the whole ocean, elevated, overtaking land." No one says. No one sings. The horizon of heat.

Spine of life rippling out of sight indistinguishable at last from the thousand tongues of death. Shining with the secular eyes of the saint. I, the unkind.

Out of silence, a thinker to be thought. Questions for the master of *Denkender*: dank thoughts of the ender, dark thanks of the child.

Misted non-site of the century's master on his mountaintop, out of death (*Todtnauberg*), out of blackness (*Schwarzwald*) and nearness (*nearness*). The accusative destroys the in-between. All that is air melts into air.

Out of the unwinding of the century and its deathbrought speech, the counter to that-which-happens, the nearly now. We live it again, encountering the WAVE.

CLOCKWISE / THE WAVE

CROSS THE STREAMS THE CENTURIES

The MASTER fixes his wing. From his mountaintop he sows. Past the POET with his hands in pockets eyes fixed on his shoes. Past HANNAH in the lowlands watching for the WAVE. The WAVE when it comes that sweeps away everything: cows factories unhappy families owls the necessity of caring about owls. The desert-jungle leaps in the night of human forgetting. Hannah sits up late in Freiburg, in Berlin, in Paris, in New York. She writes letters to the MASTER that she does not post. The eagle stands on the postmark single-headed bearing the symbol of the sun in its claws. The sun we have invited too close to the earth. It presses out the sky. No gods any more. The POET invites the rivers that flow from every direction to the sea. The beach, the moon. The desert-jungle is near, it surrounds everyone's breathing. Not so careful of the type, thinks the PLAGIARIST, who is the POET's secret face. The face of terrified complicity. The ash from HANNAH's cigarette. She writes from the night of tears in a language not her own. The CALIBRATOR listens in his bulletproof box. Listening across oceans for the WAVE that a POET can name. Its origins as wall as water as soft targeted array as emigrant flesh, mad X of the world. While the MASTER soars, terrible and blind, in the wake of the larger predator named BEING.

FIRST LOVE

HANNAH is young but she understands the MASTER
will never leave his wife. His eyes
follow when, naked, she rises from the bed
and squats over the pail
they must use for a chamber pot
in his cabin in the woods.
He listens to the trickle of her urine
in the dark, sees her teeth flash,
smiling. Now
when she stands she is a pale small acre
and the black triangle of hair at his eye level
darker than the dark that surrounds them.
Sweet halo of adulterous night.
He opens his arms to her, white and fleshy, says something
in German. Of course it's their native language:
as babies their mothers each cradled their sweet tallow heads
singing *Schlaf, Kindlein, schlaf*. Shadows
what the sun would mark.
She gives herself to him, that night and forever after.
Across murderous oceans
an endless self-erosion that penetrated from beyond.
She gives herself to him and decades after, an old man,
he has only to close his dark large lustrous eyes
to see nothing.

The innocuous accusative, the destroyer.

MAR CITY

The MASTER lectures on concealment and truth.
The POET coughs badly in the night of his work detail
and the PLAGIARIST sits smiling
at the edge of his daughter's bed, watching her sleep.
The MASTER writes *being* on the board in yellow chalk
with a small b. HANNAH smokes
in a café somewhere, gesticulating, arguing
with Husband Number One. The animals hold their breath.
They are waiting to drop out of their trees
into holes. They are waiting for the desert-jungle.
For Lake Michigan to drain away, revealing
mourning accomplished. I eat a sandwich.
The MASTER eats a sandwich.
The POET wants a sandwich.
The PLAGIARIST is starving.
Feed a cold, starve a fever:
starve the fever of the WAVE.
HANNAH as a very young girl, skipping her way to school.
The MASTER was an altar boy.
The POET remains the POET.
The PLAGIARIST mounts the barricades and urges the mob
to murder his stepfather, the CALIBRATOR.
The CALIBRATOR and his whores
dance across a tabletop in the moonlight,
scattering the figurines of the civilian population.
Tanned and resting his flaccid cock on the table's edge.
In a cloud of invisible smoke
from the bones of dinosaurs
the CALIBRATOR is serviced by women in the masks of animals,
with heads like donkeys, elephants, armadillos, and owls.
Ontic thought hops from head to head
like matches taking flame; the
shabby heart of *Shabbat* lights

a winter in every week.
It takes countable weeks to do the work of the WAVE
and the CALIBRATOR's eyes cross when he comes.

A rapture life.
400+ parts per million.
The world eats the earth, the earth eats the world.

EXTERIOR CENTURY

The past tucked neatly inside the present, like the strip of paper in a fortune cookie. The past we repeat as neither tragedy nor farce, but as plagiarism. I claim those times as my own. As Marcel painstakingly reconstructs his own fatal naivete, his only possibility for grasping time, reaching always toward the final revisionary volume. In something as cheap as a cookie the whole past can be folded and come rising up again in the body like a WAVE. Like the paper wrapper on a straw coiled down and expanded by water, snake of the world on a formica table, expanding. Towering brimful to the top of my skull. To the tip of a pyramid of skulls. Who foresaw the WAVE. Who named the promised land. Who came to the brink of that land and rallied the troops, who killed their way in, while he watched from the mountaintop, wavering in extreme old age, remembering bearded ones: *You must not see My face.* Who died, landless. Broken under the WAVE or atop it, either way a function of its structure, a soliton. One half of totalitarianism is terror. The other half is the police. They arrest the mind in its flight and send it reeling: the Black lives. Many blue arms, arbitrary. Many games of blindman's buff, many many room 101s. HANNAH sent reeling into the arms of the MASTER and out again, a tango that spins her out, far out, out of her very language. Wordless and worldless. WAVE out of Hokusai out of Mexico out of *Anschluss* hovering over her left shoulder. Far into the night, over the heavy metal desks of mid-century, she writes. While the MASTER hunkers in his hut, smooths his mustache, licks his thumb, turns the page.

---

sneering: the POET's *pasarán*, his *peace
to the cottages!*

EXTERIOR TELEVISION

I wish to say a word for middle age, for the heyday in the blood tamed and cooling, for carbon blowing midway to disaster on Mauna Loa, for the heart of heartlessness, the self's immigrant turned away. I wish to say that midway through our life's journey we have misplaced literacy, the soul, right terror for angels. For a while they carried us, those characters, the survivors. We discovered with them the island. We discovered the conspiracy against boredom and acedia riding a secret submarine. Oppen: *Crusoe // We say was / "Rescued."* We learned how to live together, conspiring. The first two or two-and-a-half seasons were great before the whole thing devolved into half-assed mystical bullshit. So unnecessary. There is nothing more mystical than a plane crash. There is nothing more mystical than unmarked cans of food. There is nothing more mystical than the Electoral College. There is nothing more mysterious than smooth flesh and a wrinkled brow, afraid of posing questions.

A child is born and the blindfold slips off. Repeat the steps of the dance.

The POET goes blind to the precipice and the PLAGIARIST guides his air-seeking feet. Down and down and down.

---

every breath you take, carbon

every word you say, carbon

NOUS SOMMES TOUS LES JUIFS ALLEMANDS

In May '68? Not bloody likely.

In the thousand-year Reich? It will end with tears.

In the twilight of the Holocene and the W A V E's false dawn?

The emigrant accused her: איו הב אפילו ושמץ של אהבת ישראל
No shred of love for her people—*Ahavath Israel*—the replicants we are.

She owns the free fall: "I merely belong to them." Asking:

Whose *we*?
Whose *all*?
Whose *German*?   (Americans)
Whose *Jews*?   (the un-)

IF WE CALLED HER DAISY

If she sat for a while in the overperfumed parlor of the twentieth century, watchful with the MASTER's corpse, the MASTER *as* corpse. Two candles set at his head, throwing shadows. Creepy. If later we discover her upstairs in her room, at home in diaspora, writing between four walls.

A camera has to show you things. DAISY can only show herself:

Weep for courtesy but
do not believe I
witness, I am masked
and dried like ink

by sand, planned
economies, a nostalgia
for them, plans.
Sometimes I crouch

low, take shelter
in doorframes
book passage
on a plane falling

from the sky: Mister,
you shook me, I spun
the records, my parents understood
loneliness and tried

for a while not to live
apart, then: death
came, a good citizen
needs a man

to call you to tell
him I don't need you
any more. Finches
and other tiny birds

they follow one another
like sparrows in a cloud:
Mister, I am alive
in time that you've forgotten

that you put away:
MASTER, I am in a dress,
I write to your evening
but will not stay.

INTERIOR NATURE

HANNAH in the garden in the cool of the evening, alone:

Don't get too mythopoetic about it. There must be place names and contingencies. There has to be a margin for the reader. Her fantasy. There has to be a sense of assembly—the opposite of mobilization. Gradually you come to participate in the story, your story. That's why I must be a woman. There are babies purpling the landscape, making it tender. There are special effects to help us see the methane, the haze, premonitory of the WAVE. There are small capitals used sparingly, there is caressing of nouns. I communicate to myself the terror. I imagine life.

"There is such a thing as a basic gratitude for everything that is as it is; for what has been *given* and was not, could not be, *made*; for things that are *physei* and not *nomo*."

Could I predict the WAVE from the postwar eddy? Redolent redoubt. From the foreclosed century?

"I said that there was no possibility of resistance, but there existed the possibility of *doing nothing.*"

The possible garden
                    the desert of carbon
                                    the jungle of capital
                                                          : against the grain.

EIN MEISTER AUS DANTE

I climbed his mountain

Out of nothing, robed in red
        (as cardinal-
        birds, as rust
        on a redbreast

Howling out the Trecento or
preserving his dignity like a lemon in sugar

        (this guest, this bride-
        groom with no bride
        nine year's glimpse
        of vita nuova a life
        in prose happiness

                between language
                and monarchy that
                is good German he

never spoke of suffering without moral cause
gave himself to wolf and wood, Ghibelline and Guelph

        (making much of me of
        forests made stranger no notion
        no nation language is
        double paired swords
        enter the heart

                bright the eye
                blinds the thinker
                hell is a city
                of orchids

I give out my story
to him in his heaven where he
reads no more.

Paradise. Off-world. The W A V E.

The POET leaps out of his nothingness.

H A N N A H : I cannot love myself or anything which I know is part and parcel of my own person.

EXTERIOR CARE

The MASTER's is a pale spreading body that he tries not to notice in the mirror: only his face where his mustache needs trimming. But in his bath it's hard to ignore that expanse of livid, bulging flesh. The curve of the belly with its many individual black and white hairs. The curl of his penis adhering to one thigh or the other. The joints where the small aches fester: knees, ankles, the massive stub of his big right toe. Under sedentary fat long muscles roll, especially in the arms that still like to swing an axe. The bald crest of the head habitually concealed by an Alemannic cap—the MASTER's *kippah*, the skull's foreskin. Though his wife grinds her teeth in her sleep when she dreams them, their feral faces, their misshapen noses, their refugee skins. More –man than the –mans, Greek to the MASTER, the *they* to the *she*. What is national in this body from which the stink of mortality will not be washed away? Though hours pass in water passing from hot to tepid to cold, floating grease. The MASTER stands resolute dripping from chin and fingertips and penis and scrotum. He wraps a towel around his middle and sticks his pipe in his mouth. It's time for a little postwar snack, a dish of sausages and a few herring. The MASTER's wife is smashing plates downstairs so he'll linger here for a bit longer buffing his buttocks dry, admiring without intention his heavy flanks in the mirror, his sunken chest, avoiding his own eyes. From somewhere below a short sharp shock of a howl, a whipped dog's cry. As smoke from the chimney of his mouth fills the smallest room of his house, lightens it like a balloon, and carries him away.

INTERIOR LETTER FROM THE MASTER

In elegance: *un ritorno*.
Bach Brandenburg Concerto no. 3
2nd movement, *allegro*

HANNAH,

I brought what is most yours closer. Right of return. For your averted gaze awakens intimacy from afar.

Time is oddly mysterious. Can we feel it: gratitude for what has become of us.

I said *du*. Love plants everything, breaks the enframing of the world.

I have her fidelity to thank, my wife.

I spoke of "beauty." Who may reach into the depths of terror, but lovers?

I need her love. I need your love. Its Phrygian cadence.

(Silent friendship.)

A fair copy of our conversation on the forest paths. In the shadow of the castle. That beauty may unite extreme opposites, intimately.

(A sort of musical semicolon.)

The gift of return and the taking stock of so many years keep intruding on my thoughts, in which, far across the sea, you are near and present, thinking yourself here toward those dearest to you and toward all the things that belong with you.

I say it again: *du*. Beauty is a form of terror as the POET said. The tortuous intimacy of towers. The depths of ordinary life from which the angels, sharklike, strike.

Her love, which bore everything in silence through the years. Love needs love.

Hannah, when the century tears at you furiously, think of the straight firs towering up before us, into the light air of midday in the winter mountains. Everywhere the colors. The other turns his back.

Your gaze, shy *fraulein*, shy *fraulein* . . . !

M.

EXTERIOR VISION

From city heights the sleeper descends, down the elevator, down the subway stairs, down into bedrock and through, down into the muffled blackness of the earth that imperceptibly at first and then completely lightens, whitens into cloud's furze, sun's halo, the scored layers of blue sky below which the dimpled hills and valleys of the forest tumble and roll.

HANNAH digs down to him through the scored layers of sky in her dream. Down and down, membrane after membrane, to the cabin roof. She would cut a hole in that roof, a skylight to admit the sky's qualities, to open the lid of thought in the roof of the cabin on the side of the mountain in the heart of the forest. Light finds the visitor's registry and blows through the history of names. The MASTER sits at a plain deal table, writing. If he looked up he would see HANNAH floating there like a jellyfish not six inches above his head, motiveless, adopting as her own the subtle movements of the air stirred by the sterile heat of a single bulb. He does not look up. His moving hand and pentip leave a trail to dazzle her retinas, trace a wake. The fox wears no fur. The jellyfish, all skirts, in her inscrutable floating life, rotating, umbilical. Rooted to this cabin, spiracle, a mote in the vast cyanotic eye of the forest. Calling: look up. Vocational. Calling: full stop squatting on top of his head. The MASTER goes on writing. HANNAH's eyes follow the track of her outstretched arms, down to the earth working in the track of turning treads, filled in behind by corpses, up again to the measuring unsheltered given of being, the home of gods and satellites, our new politics, the steel horizon, the sky.

THE SHIELDS / *LOVE* SONGS

OF HANNAH R.

Every time she leaves that long, dreamy, unyielding sleep, in which one is so entirely oneself, as if at one with what one dreams, she lost the same shy and groping tenderness for the things of the world in which she had become aware of a great part of her real life—absorbed in sleepiness, one might say, as if from her ordinary life something comparable had fled. For strangeness and tenderness had loomed early in her life, threatening her identity. Tenderness meant shy, restrained affection, not the giving of oneself but a sounding, the caressing astonishment of strange forms.

INVOCATION

Some where so ever
blood whitely flies
its whole dish in kissing,
you never more than missing—

we're swollen unfrozen.
Gas harbors wine,
gas floats the linden
and the unexamined find.

When letters fail us
that lass outside
goes nuts underwater
where her mission's mislaid.

The wrongs you take upon yourself, like logs, across one's own shoulders.

Burden of our times.

Bur(de)ning.

Maybe it all stemmed from the fact that in her quietest, barely youthful youth she had already stumbled upon something extraordinary and wonderful, and so later came the almost self-evident habit of duplicating her life: in the here and now, the then and there. I don't mean longing for a particular thing—that is too limited—but the desire for what makes a life can in itself become what composes it.

UNTITLED

Kind foot bright in under—
Kind god helps his hand—
Foreign is the brick
Terminal the land.

Kind form of the loser,
Kind shadow of the swept.
Immersed makes not a whore
Too late, too late.

But nothing destroys so radically the condition of equality, the foundation of human relationships, than forgiveness. Its abandon.

It was as though her independent and bizarre nature were manifested by what inspired in her the truest, most peculiar passion, so used to seeing in even the most ordinary and banal things something noteworthy; yes, it went this far, that even when she recognized the simplicity and ordinariness of her own life, it did not occur to her to recognize that an encounter might be trivial, something with which all the world is familiar and of which it never pays to speak.

TRUST

It's come to stand
The old wound.
The lanced forgotten.
The droned refreshed.

It's come undone.
That little wage
Destroys our living
Without enterprise.

Understand whatever
The days undergo—
It's blindly winning
The bested, blessed.

---

child of the only child
                        in thought

But nothing of that kind has ever been made explicit. The sky in the city in which she grew up imposed itself on her, irresolute and immobilized. She had many wishes, was always on the alert for experience. But everything that happened to her dropped to the bottom of her soul and remained there, isolated and encapsulated. Her lack of resolve and unrestraint prevented her from meeting events with anything but dull pain or a dreamy, enchanted exaltedness. So she did not know how to do anything, hardly even looking after herself; although, yes, one could speak of her bewilderment, which naturally led to greater and greater absurdities. The deeper and, to a degree, the more thoroughgoing she became, the less she understood, least of all of herself. It was not as if she had forgotten something; rather, she had literally sunk, like someone lost, one more dull rebel lacking discipline and organization.

TRAUM

Swaybacked first by pathetic glances,
It is self.
Out of trances
Befitting one who swerves.
Indicative, his leer.
Bedraggled room where strangers' ersatz
Door-scribbles whiten
Forlorn *Einsatzgruppen*
Beginning their trance, their dance.

He is self
Out of the I's trance.
Ironic for the mess
Leaves no night guessing.
I meet his leer,
I know his smear,
I dance, I trance
His ironical glance.

What Husband Number One might say:

we are living in the Age of Inability to Fear

thy neighbor as thyself

Her devastation, caused perhaps only by her helpless, betrayed youth, was expressed in this passage—isolated, depressed—in such a way that she disguised and obscured her own gaze, her own access to herself. The doubleness of her essence was so apparent that it obstructed itself. The longer it persisted, the more she became radical, exclusive, and blind.

MUD KITE

Damn the end and the ends—
Leave all clarity
Taunt notch the focal ruff
Of the eyes, enough.

Grave fainter,
Fallen her leader,
My hand and taint
Finds him wider.

What is belief?
Can I nothing fasten?
What makes ugly
Can I no way lose.

All sinks
Dammed straight off.
Hissed missile winks—
His will his life his laugh.

---

we, after all, the public thing

continuously tries to visualize

the chance of truth

In stupidity, in inhumanity, in absurdity, she found neither limit nor foothold. A radicality that always went to extremes did not protect her, went unarmed, never gave her even the bitterest dregs from the emptiest cup. The best came to a bad end, the worst to a good end. Hard to say which was more unbearable. For yes, it is just that which is the most unbearable that takes your breath away, the limitless fear one thinks of, the horror that one can only avoid and prevent by staying at home. To suffer and to know, in every minute and second, that one is to thank even the worst pain; yes, that even this suffering is something for which to be grateful.

THE UNDERGROUND

House or dunce commands
In his hell such slain geldings:
Snow and permission,
Smally the essence
Of fundamental likeness, craft.
Irksome verdancy
Gets eyes out of the way.
Bright guilt we bend
Outward then hasten.

Snow, small essence
Of manly craftiness:
He is nothing's architect
In a dank flea's end.
Bear us, whistling:
Fleet of such intent
In guilt we fear.

Since work is action in disguise

                what can be used will be used

                              : leave nothing in the ground

Sophistication and taste were no refuge. What was worthwhile, what did anything matter when everyone declined to strike at the defenseless one who belonged nowhere and never had? Her sensitivity and vulnerability, which has always given her something exclusive, had become something nearly grotesque. An animal fear—for she neither was able nor desired to protect herself—coupled with a matter-of-fact expectation of insult made the simplest and most natural things in life more and more impossible.

OH SHIT

None last night, O swimming beggar, handed you wrecks.
Their intent more likely was giving kind advice
Instead of twice losing.

Each leg is glued when the friends there frighten
Signs varied a bit, if will knits and whitens—
In the rear chapter, heighten.

Oh dear can that lack in me then mix and shank me?
They're worsened by fields if divided for hanging.
Um. Out of reason you lead: and each you's for whoring.

Dark jets roofed that blued, that nearer entangled
Hint mixed from sleep, that animals lent.
The toad is in labor, it's white, it's white.

So last night, O swimming beggar, the hand of you wrecked
Where farriers might mix. If less than the sum tightens
This bladder in flame, unstuck.

---

identifiable and visible objects of hatred will be exhibited,
                                        in emergency cases invented—

"Jews" of all kinds.

I have published these words in order to prevent them from becoming true.

In the bitterly shy early morning of her young life, when she had yet to quarrel with the tentative tender manner of expression of her own peculiar nature, she had through sorrow discovered realms of reality in her dreams—those sorrowful and joyful dreams that are filled with a constant vitality whether they are sweet or bitter. Later, in a strange, violently destructive act of self-domination, she spoiled her youth, rejecting it as an inadequate lie; she abandoned restraint for a hypnotic fear of reality, an utterly meaningless empty fear, before whose blind gaze everything becomes nothing, which means madness, joylessness, oppression, annihilation. This fear is no more terrible or deadly than one's own reflection. This is her character, and at the same time, the sign of her shame. But what should you find more horrible or incomprehensible than your own reality?

IN SUCH I'VE SUNKEN

When what my hand betrays
—Friends ring if they're fervent—
Stays in its kindly land,
Being unkind here and yet
Being kind as one was beset.

Damnation more or less salt in the welt retracting
Mad dogs ruing the day's fair gains
Nor swollen like strychnine but more unseen.

Be wracked in my hand,
Unhomelike near my fair want.
And of the other thing:
If she's more or less me
Hates she hearing since?

We cannot translate the senses: the heard cannot be an image for the eye, the seen cannot adequately be represented by the word. "The eye of man hath not heard."

The pictures of the Greeks, the letters of the Jews: they ban one another.

The untranslatable transcends. But we,
                                  the plural,
                                               need a world.

She had succumbed to fear as she had once succumbed to longing—not to a fear of anything in particular but to the fear of existence itself. She had known it before, as she had known so many things that had befallen her.

SUMMER LEAD

Dirt this summer's rival filled.
Glassy my hemmed, lightened
My bleeder, smashed by the
Too suddenly smeared air.

Felt her disease turn, nighten
Felt pads of what's walled, shooting
Alice, the Sphinx, some strange strident
That. We're living when we're dying.

That's that other, that's defilement
Since his priestly hand's forlorn,
That the elder, clearer still
Sends me j o y a n c e, nicked, a star.

Then the washer fleeces over:
Muddy kites will us restore
What's for lashing unseriously
When we're praying, when we're prey.

Wrongs
cleaned
Forgiveness
Revenge
Reconciliation
Inequality
Reality
Opportunity
has
done
permitted
radical Evil
Revenge

                                                       "My life closed twice before its close"

Maybe the transformation of yearning into fear through destructive domination, the slavish tyranny of the self-rapist, can be understood by considering that even the monstrous possibilities went neglected in a hopeless time, all the more so given her sharply self-conscious, highly cultivated and picky tastes that resisted the increasingly loud and desperate attempts at art, literature, and culture, clawing carelessly at the most absurd disputes to the point of shamelessness.

UNTITLED

Far from gifts you mar my hand
Shy and free, like goyim?
Coming to us so far from land
Can nothing sear the vine?

Can nothing scare some shunned glut
(Leaps too are aligned)
Mesdames / und Herren, in the blood,
Ice the other sign?

Why'd you miss this haggard friend
With the leapster's game,
Why'd you skip the abject, snide
Dance, its snare, its beam?

Come what's near and have my lip
Thank what's in the ground,
Can't your dick then switch around?
Come and name and give.

Gain what the rifle felt
(Moan and fill their glee)
Bait her in her wider welt
All hurts on the way.

When we're spooning we invent
Stark interesting wait;
In the shower dream's laugh lift
Under its zeal, the weight.

"This is the reason,
                and the only reason,
                              you must hang."

~~But this is only an attempt to explain the cause, to bring humanity somewhat closer to the private and the intimate. The real possibility of this despair in the realm of the human opens its eyes in every moment, and it is only for that reason that the threatening, ghostlike nature of the process can be understood.~~

BAIT SUMMER

The ardent had made you architect
So white we sank somewhere we laid.

Advise no more we leave it taut,
Advise no more to field her boot,
And all will enter laden
And no more air will gape in.

I stink of him and have been led
From where? As softened, landed.
And fretted with my come and give
Calm wiseguy was what banged.

The abject had made you predict
That what we sank was where we laid.
And nervous as an imperial wreck
You knew your friend and liked it.

And all averted like relief
And all the guests' clear white teeth
Can't picnic more before then.

If wise in water grows a friend,
Denies a bloom that cannot mend
What sail will not restore me?

The event has made you architect
But while we sat, some werewolf lied.

. . . the singing poem, which removes and releases what it sings from the in-between and its relations, without confirming anything.

It may be that, as yearning increases the fear of being lost or addicted, this rigid adherence to the one thing also decays. The empty gaze forgets the variety of objects, or does not care for anything, filled only by addiction and passion. Maybe longing had disclosed to her a realm, a colorful and peculiar kingdom in which she was at home, and in which she could love with that everlasting vitality that fear shut up, that beheaded free breath and rigidified in pursuit. If it must be emphasized that this made her uglier and more ordinary, to the point of stolid slovenliness, so be it— but then only the freedom of indifference could stand up to the weight of rectitude.

ANTIFINDER

Throw it—not the lesser crag.
What's unbuilt this time-out lessens
Short of nothing, inverted.
Fooled, we stole the rancid sage—
All is not forgiving.

Spurt the dank bark white and try
Star systems or bait them.
And enlist in state the new
Word the believer gave them.

---

the exact opposite of vengeance

                                                re-[en]acting against

                                                                                                    an original trespassing

The numbness of the hunted—so that joy and sorrow, pain and despair, fled through her as if through dead flesh—evaporated all reality, ricocheting through the present so that the only certainty was that everything had to end. Her radicality, which once held and carried her, had changed so that she now tore and destroyed everything, though she tried to cling to an appearance of docile kindness, pale and colorless with the secret fear of one whose path scurried into shadow.

ANTINAUGHT

Neither too trusting in my own hurting
Sinking my divided lingering in their singing
Decking my shield for all who are hell—
Get nearer, hermit, and flood your own grill.

Let mere dungeons cool you in loss,
Let me in darkness foreignness dispose.
Then hell makes pain a gnawing proposition;
Give up my craft to state its transcription.

To live with the me myself
                                                     not

                                                               to want

                                                                                to share

                                                                                                the earth

                                                                                                                       with you

It is yet possible that her youth will break free from the spell, and her soul, under another sky, will experience the possibilities of speech and solution, thus overcoming illness and perversity, learning patience at last, and the simplicity and freedom of organic growth. But it's more likely that she will continue to spend her life in baseless experiments and bottomless curiosity, until finally the long and devoutly to be wished end takes her by surprise, putting an end to her purposelessness.

Königsberg i/Pr., April 1925
Persönlich für M.H.

W.B.

    Once damned and bent we dare
    Not fail the needle fundamental,
    Lead there, a district bleeder
    In denial, in the foreign.

    Out of the dungeon's tone
    Zaftig, climb melodies.
    Lazarused we're entering
    The locked ending we're denying.

    Fair stitching, never comes our
    Yearning sting, a leaner total;
    Deviate from *Blut und Boden*
    And you lighten after summer.

Of the anti-MASTER let it last be said:

Si vivi vicissent qui morte vicerunt

COUNTERCLOCKWISE

\ *VOIGT-*KAMPFF

INTERIOR BUNKER THE COUNTER-CENTURY

Widescreen nativity: nativity of the eye. Ringed by lashes and flames.

Endgame cinema, Nuremberg hypothesis, the present unforgiven by both past and future.

The horizontal city lights its depths without benefit of computers or clergy. Visible pulse of infrastructure pulsing the skin of buildings, falling cars, the ruined sky, the people navigating a climax climate signified by the endlessness of the dirty rain.

Spectacularly decaptured carbon conceals/reveals the vertical. Gods of biomechanics lounge aside from the clinamen disclaiming the desert-jungle. Ice ages of the mind.

INTERIOR pyramid's primal scene of the masked and goggled DOCTOR in mint-green scrubs poised over cellular vats delicately inserting eyeballs into needful heads. Encased in nutrient slime quintessential bodies of the century remade for the new world, the counter-century. Cackling in his MASTER's voice: *Man encounters only himself.*

Man-form and woman-form drip-dry on metal benches in the night of postmodern poetry. Then led almost quiescent by gloved hands into habitats, monochrome simulacra of the century we cannot kiss goodbye.

HIS cabin in the sky simulates a mountaintop. Clinical hands dress him, furnish the necessary skullcap, white collar, black notebooks, pen and desk. Pose him alone under dark leaves to fulfill his function. HE does.

SHE in the cloister looking into a yard populated by artificial birds having dressed herself simply in blouse, skirt, stockings, shoes. Ashtray, cigarette, typewriter. Eyes alight with their own smoke. SHE thinks.

Diorama splitscreen his and hers watched by the DOCTOR reclined in the sublime of replication, its infinite count simulating abundance. At his elbow the implants, so many historical paper dolls.

Ripple affect of hearing through the lens of the screen the work of thought that is almost prayer.

When the film ends, history ends with it. A tale to be told in the aftermath of life as we know it.

Crossing the cinematic boundary, before the twentieth century is implanted in their bodies, the blank of SHE and the blank of HE meet. SHE lies her head in HIS lap and HE strokes HER hair, absently. With his other hand HE writes:

Night of the worldless and the human Jews.

Night of the furies of repetition.

Night of depleted uranium ideologies. Night of the future enframed by a lost logic of exploitation.

Cinema of night. Shock of light. Its artificial day.

FADE IN:

AFFIDAVIT OF IDENTITY IN LIEU OF A PASSPORT

We must bring up the bodies, the bodies, clinically wrapped, measured, and screened.

The MASTER, a basic pleasure model
Talk about beauty and the beast: he's both
Optimum self-sufficiency
A nuclear loader

HANNAH in her youth black-clad, steady of gaze, cradling herself with one hand and a cigarette with the other, bright line of buttons stalking down the center of her dress. Watchful, iconic becoming.

I, JOHANNAH BLUCHER, nee Arendt, also known as HANNAH ARENDT residing at 130 Morningside Drive, New York 27, N.Y.
being duly sworn, depose and state:

1. I was born on Oct. 14, 1906 at Hannover in Germany
2. My occupation is Writer; Executive Secretary of Jewish Cultural Reconstruction, Inc.
3. I am married; the name of my husband is Heinrich Blucher born on Jan. 29, 1899 at Berlin/Germany   , residing at 130 Morningside Drive, New York 27, N.Y.

4. I am a former citizen of Germany   and at present stateless

10. I am attaching hereto my photograph and I am giving my personal description as evidence of my identity.

There the image truly creased. Signature of statelessness, signature of suffering, sutured to her name:

[signature: Hannah Blücher – Arendt]

The work of fiction. The Thirties, the Forties, sea levels of anti-Semitism. Statelessness stalks us in the night of the WAVE, its climax architecture. Six degrees centigrade by 2100. The century unravels before then, winding backward by rapid degrees: drains of capital, new feudalisms, primitive deaccumulation, renewing the solitude of the earth.

From *all sorrows must be borne* to *all sorrows can be borne*—

Naïve survivals at home in species-being—

Stamped return to sender—

Stamped *pleasure model* – "I think, therefore I am—"

"Very good, now show him why."

Why is vector feeling: "feeling from a beyond which is determinate and pointing to a beyond which is to be determined." Alfred North Whitehead, *Process and Reality*.

Pleasure, which is fundamentally the intensified awareness of reality.

Stamped sealed delivered—

Papers for citizens of the counter-century,

                                      for zugzwang, light's stale-

                                                                         mate:

I am a survivor, and not intact.

BANALITY OF DAYS

Days like any others, the disaster touching down elsewhere, with increasing frequency. We are spared?

Men are accomplices to that which leaves them indifferent.

Am I the Eichmann of the WAVE? The gentile of the desert-jungle?

Imaginary evil is romantic and varied; real evil is gloomy, monotonous, barren, boring.

The CALIBRATOR, the aligner, the buffoon. There is no alias for him, no algebra, no *nom de plume*.

Kidnapped from the dream of off-world colonies into the desert-jungle of the now.

When we recommend the opposite of an evil we remain on the level of that evil.

In this simulation he sits there in his glass box, bent under the weight of black headphones whispering the gap between Hebrew and German. Look at HANNAH, similarly encumbered, listening, frowning, bent to her pages. The phrase is hovering outside the bounds of what her pen will record, on the tip of her tongue. Not the banality of blank but the blank of _____. The lapse into the formlessness of filling out forms. The sinister redistribution of agency that his trial, the record of that trial, will mark. (*Eich* means "calibration.") While fingers are still on buttons. (*Mann* does not mean "man.") While carbon chokes the sky in the name of freedom (*the Soviets plus electrification*), invisibly blocking views of G-D.

EXTERIOR JERUSALEM: *DER PROZESS*

At last you are *fed up with being an anonymous wanderer between the worlds.*

This incident kept bothering him. *Times have changed so much.*

An idealist was a man who lived for his idea.

It hurt him *to hurt their feelings*, this Eichmann, this anti-Bartleby who will never *prefer*.

His heroic fight with the German language, which invariably defeats him. *Officialese is my only language.*

A single sentence that was not a cliché.

Quite an unwholesome book: Lolita.

Often thoughts which, though hideous
      word for word
were not empty.

Against reality as such.

His sympathy for a hard-luck story.

My years-long efforts to obtain land and soil
Everything was as if under an evil spell
I was frustrated in everything, no matter what
suddenly stuttering with rage a mechanism
      that had become completely unalterable.

It was normal and human
all his grief and sorrow.
Keep the gravel paths in order

a great inner joy to me
not gassed, apparently, but shot.

Is this bad faith, or outrageous stupidity? Winds of Mauna Loa.

I never met a single man who would admit that he had done wrong.

Robert N. Proctor: "If ours is an age of ecology, then perhaps we should rechristen Germany in the 1930s and 1940s 'The Age of Jews.'"

Who cannot afford to face reality
       (mass extinctions)
because his crime has become part and parcel of it?

For he and the world he lived in had been once in perfect harmony.

Shielded against reality and factuality, "evil flies from the light."

A moral prerequisite for survival

The aura of systematic mendacity

extraordinary sense of elation

filled to the brim with such sentences, a different elating cliché

I will jump into my grave laughing!

It was essential that one take him seriously, and this was very hard to do.

One of the few gifts fate bestowed upon me is a capacity for truth insofar as it depends upon myself.

In full possession of my physical and psychological freedom—

his plea for mercy
changing moods
this horrible gift for consoling

                                              Raus
                                              Rein
                                              Raum

                                                                     the world without us

(Master and *volk*: *ego* non *cogito ergo sum*)

We have been to the limit. We have reached the final boundary, "stepping," the POET says, "into a realm which is turned toward the human, but uncanny—"

                              (more human than
                    human

                                                          (the again and
                                                            again

Here for the first and last time I had a choice.

Yes, he had a conscience.

[ ] in the coming winter could no longer be fed. These things sound sometimes fantastic, but they are quite feasible.

[ ]

The native animalized hordes. A destroyer of human beings or an annihilator of culture?

Her "shy, resolute persistence" in the face of her own replication.

Happily the survivors—

Happily—

No century for them now—

WORDS DEEP DOWN IN THE SEA

The DOCTOR's underwater LABORATORY. Apparatus climb the walls, metal beds with drains, switches and dials and scurrying rats, Bunsen burners and Jacob's Ladders, electricity climbing to the ceiling.

The DOCTOR's rubber red hands. He speaks:

A replicant is a materialist emanation: copy of a copy of a copy of the Form Divine.

Commerce is our goal and a genetic copy, as with the digital, suffers no degradation in resolution or quality.

"More human than human"? That's just something we say. To live is to choose . . . something else.

Replication circumvents birth, implies—wrongly—a perfect origin and a given understanding.

Out of Albion, Los Angeles, Europa, toward nexus and Atlantis. Survivors of the artifice, cresters of the WAVE. It's my madness to return them to the world.

Only poets like beggars still celebrate birth. We work in the dark, uncovenanted, bookless.

Poets who sin against distance, bringing the spark of their own lives near, emanations of the unseen, forbidden earth.

The replicant, other to itself, implanted in a history not its own, opens a space to be detonated by a You.

I'm not a replicant. I'm Klaus Kinski.

I do not challenge my times, the that-which-happens. I *turn*.

A stranger to nature, I am the mother of wounds. That grow, and speak, and remember themselves.

The female forms.

I serve the MASTER that I made.

HANNAHLIEDER / *RED* THREAD

DO (YOU)

    Worser phlegm—flame—frame—
    For you I take fright.
    Dot dit dot—
    and disentangle
    sudden buyers
    of still waters
    —essential reef—
    feeder and finder of such valors.

"the worser flame"

A few Greek letters like wounds in the earth. "Fields of memory and devotion."

Speech in her mouth, lent him for a day. A wish (*wunsch*) not in her power to grant.

Habits of mind of the poetry she learned of him. The cognates and false friends. The illusory etymology of *depth*:

[Old English *deop* (adjective), *diope, deope* (adverb), of Germanic origin; related to Dutch *diep* ānd German *tief*: s̄ynonȳms *hoch* (lofty), *stark* (intense, profound, heavily), *dunkel* (dark), *tiefgründig* (profound), *groß* (large, big, copious, capital, large-scale, grand, keen).]

73

At the still point in the counter-century, preparing the next disaster,

    the discarded M A S T E R—

                                                    no way

      out

                                           Kein

        kehre

                       of this love

THANKING

Once against him the blitz designs
its thinking
then, phoneme publishing
slacked us of the futile [feudal]
vortext: black and white
dies, need deposits
such overwhelmings
out of cruising
one-two,
forbidden raven.
She enters, bends
an inheritor:
she hurts him then, in the word.

And it was told the king of Jericho, saying: "Behold, there came men in hither to-night of the War Boys of Israel to search out the land."

MARCH AND FANG

For H.

If I bared it, signed, answered!
If I owned it out here.
They bluen. In tears,
where croon the vines,
trunks of drunkards without wines.

R. was a harlot and innkeeper:

But she had brought them up to the roof, and hid them with the stalks of flax, which she had spread out upon the roof.

THEIR ROOF

In fairness gangs of naiads
won't
show
their wild jars—
mild flickers
inside underwhelming knickers.
Then *she* knows more.
This then the roof of horns
           "surrender"
Doubt big
things, we're
where science relents.

And she said to the War Boys, "I know that G-D hath given you the land, and that your terror is fallen upon us, and that all the inhabitants of the earth melt away before you.

VELDT

In touching their looks
though giving
ruin each gesture—
state your hurt
see it rise—
gated bereavement
surrounding a release
and bow to nothingness.

"For we have heard how G-D dried up the water."

"HOLES, WAYS"

For H.

Last here, you're naming
here and there
your own fear:

to free her same
sane life,
her griefs

where wary welcome to
the earth comes
in glut, the front

(the fineness of things working, but under carbon, well . . .)

"And as soon as we had heard it, our hearts did melt, neither did there remain any
more spirit in any man, because of you . . . "

MADE THEN OUT THE FRAME

The frame,
the self-same frame
she is:
given to winning
merely these leads
westerly furlongs
frolicked and answered.
Framed: homogenous blacks
where wealth begins.
Begin to open.
Operas suss no lord of truth,
not all is brained.
Ash under-glimpsed and
wounded.
Good her meal,
shined her steel.
Fraulein unframed, do
you own or begin.

And the War Boys said unto her, "Our life for yours, if ye tell not this our business; and it shall be, when G-D giveth us the land, that we will deal kindly and truly with thee."

OWN TATTLE: RENDERING

In your end, raring (rearing) bits of mine.
Veer a spade's warning: in the schwingmoor,

Schindanger,

knacker's yard,

fall in.

———————————————————————

Then she let them down by a cord through the window.

DIVORCÉE

G-D lost that good
ally, sunshine
there dingy
where either toad
springs in or
out the ring.
I am through getting it.
Those are signs.

"Behold, when we come into the land, thou shalt bind this line of scarlet thread in the window which thou didst let us down by; and thou shalt gather unto thee in the house thy father, and thy mother, and thy brethren, and all thy father's household.

"And it shall be, that whosoever shall go out of the doors of thy house into the street, his blood shall be upon his head, and we shall be guiltless; and whosoever shall be with thee in the house, his blood shall be on our head, if any hand be upon him."

MODE

    To list the getting-bigger of signs,
    the giving of welts.
    To entreat dimes and mines,
    answer wicks that fail.
    In a whore there's rue
    rhyming stars' unearthly truce:

            fur of the friend, the unfriended.

    And the War Boys said unto JOSHUA: "Truly G-D hath delivered into our hands all the land, and moreover all the inhabitants of the land do melt away before us."

MEN**TION**

    Where can't this style that such wealth engenders?
    Where waits your won-in, your Kodak enlightenment?
    What refts your way, in whose duty
    we are final?
    What enters speaking
    then gets it?

And they burnt the city with fire, and all that was therein.

UNDER THE WAVE

Steers out what ends our garden
near the enemy very derelict.
        That unalien carbon might fade—
        this is heaven our reigning road.
        Inert warrior I've become:
                my error your furor your kindly show
                where the quick terrors clang—
                amend them, in ichor, for saying.

But R. the harlot, and her father's household, and all that she had, did JOSHUA save alive

DISTURB AND LIKEN

Handcuffed since we've
gone to wealth-spill,
clang out of snows
sang out of fields'
wreckage: blind sheer
bang in her raging.

And she dwelt in the midst of ISRAEL, unto this day; because she hid the messengers.

PERSONA

    Your voltage forced easily your person
    and wistfully designed a tone—
    first clings what my mustache builds:
        fertile detonation
        still owns the will—
        melting atones
        while islands are forsaken—
        how I never guessed my ground
        forced high my forcing blindness.

Red thread. I would follow the fire out of fire.

A replicant's poems, like his photographs, mean nothing. Copies of copies.

In the digital regime of the counter-century without original.

No depths, only time wound like a cord inside and against time, tightly and more tightly. History repeats, a mouth.

History teaches history teaches—

FIVE-YEAR PLANS

                    H. bears me merely

Is it then dice
over where form [Form]
is getting each site
caught in vice
always stilting sternly
where golden herbs alight?

G-D said that ALL the Canaanites must perish. But HE preserved R. alive.

The rabbis say she atoned for her sins of the thigh by her thigh, by marrying JOSHUA.

Out of that-which-happened and a civilization dying by fire she wrote her name to the future.

OWN TITLE

Worsen or watch for these verdicts [these voiceless]?
Bang hearts next that were still.
A savior comes first, he's not too bright.
Language ruins him and his quell.

───

R. retires into a renewable resource. Pull yourself out of the fire, else your blood be on the hands of War Boys and of men.

Night of the WAVE, fire of the word.

BLACK HORIZONS

That's right. Arising.
Outline and lighten
its velvet get-up.
Who blabbed it out
from them, their shout?
      That mad hat fleeing
      the ear of a shoe
      her hair believes
and untried her underwear
for a trousseau,
getting testy testimony
in the sugar of not finding out
when the young one she was, winding
in the trance of second self.

Line. Lighting. Out of hand, therefore his own lass's
      οὐσία
Loud. Louding. Breaking what's still and shaming
      her still:
      Shaming the stillness of the sameness of the student's
      λόγος

οὐσία : being, substance, essence, accident

      v.

λόγος : a ground, a plea, a word, a reason

The DOCTOR hides one in the other. HANNAH waltzes with the MASTER.

Bleached coral of their lips . . .

The stillness of the century's eternal return . . .

His love unravels her world . . . .

HANNAH ARIA

You frame sudden valors

Thanking the futile vortext hurts the word

March bared, blues without wines

Their wild jars surrender science

Veldt looks, giving gesture, hurt

Rise, bereavement: release nothingness

Ways fear to free the earth

Made then frame; frame wealth, not all

Ash shined unframed

Tattle rendering fall

Down a cord, divorce G-D, that sun springs signs

Mode: whore's truce

Fur of the friend

Men: we are final?

Garden, carbon, error, terror. Amend ichor

Like hand to wealth sand wreckage in her

Your person designed the will, atones while forcing blindness

H: dice getting vice, always golden light

Voiceless title. Hearts. A too-bright language

Black horizons arising lighten the testimony in the sugar of not finding out

Lighting. Louding

The stillness of sameness.

COUNTERCLOCKWISE \ *SAINT* WORLD

INTERIOR

Description of a space. A cylinder, a room, all white or all black. Reversible, a negative of itself. Sound in the room, of the room. A body bound to a chair: mine. A swinging lamp: yours. Angels and omnivores snicker at a distance. Only thoughts in the room. Only the chair, a table, a glass of water. If there was a door by which to enter I've forgotten where to look for it. Only the room. And the films, black and white and silent, projected onto the wall behind the figure in the chair, onto the figure in the chair. So to open my eyes is to revel in his blindness. To look down to see others' bodies projected onto mine. As for the MASTER he is across seas as usual, pitying me in the light. To be so exposed, he thinks, so naked, torn so furiously by public eyes. Sealed for years after his death. A room, a cylinder or space. Planetary, in cleared space, I wander over the face of things. I fight to the front, I fight for the jungle of the visible.

SW: "And now we see them committed irretrievably to chance; suddenly things cease to obey them."

BLACK BOX

Black box of the earth. Feed it quarters the color of itself, lightless. It gives back wild heat, deodand of itself, the fire that scorches our hands, that burns our faces and leaves them without feature. We are left to be articulated in a white voice of repetition, a GIF. The spectacle unfolds from the earth and collapses everything into it. And so HANNAH forbids the sky.

The black box as invulnerable trace. DO NOT OPEN. Its doubleness as voice recorder, as record of the instruments: all that has been spoken, all that has been measured, every second of the past: now. Grain of dates, of data. NO STEP. In the hangar the investigators pace off the fuselage, the wings, puzzling the wreckage: pieces of aluminum, a single engine, the frames of the seats. The plane, its crew and passengers, exist only in the virtual space of the problem the wreckage poses, how it came to be here, displacing the arduously attained illusions of forty thousand feet, of ordinary life sustained by an infrastructure of the impossible.

The black box is orange, it is yellow, it is spherical. It pulses under the water, faintly and more faintly.

Futurity is a condition of the visible. At what age did I become conscious of the possibility of nuclear war? Five? Seven? At what point was the imaginable replaced by the inevitable? Elementary school fallout drills. A concrete corridor. The yellow sign. Does no one remember how it happened? That which happens? The predicate ending of the world?

Coiling through the dead land the snake shoots a bullet at itself, its own tail, the end.

SW: "At the outset, at the embarkation, their hearts are light, as hearts always are if you have a large force on your side and nothing but space to oppose you."

HANNAH AND HANNAH R.

— I don't approve of apocalypse narratives. Or visions.
— Just listen. I was sitting on the toilet when the roof peeled away. And I saw . . .
— I don't care what you saw. You're here, aren't you? Life goes on. In spite of everything, life goes on.
— The sky was green, Hannah. Green and cloudless. I felt two opposite feelings. That I was at the center, the absolute center, of the storm, which was the center of the universe. And at the same time I was alone, completely alone, at the margin of everything. Not even part of what was happening. Just my eyes, seeing.
— Try to be a little dialectical, can't you? The margin *is* the center, its royal road. And a visionary, if that's what you are, is practically by definition an outsider who experiences a momentary apprehension of the whole. But that's not the essential point.
— It is to me. Hannah, I saw the sky split open, only it wasn't the sky it was the earth. And I saw terrible things. Children. I won't try to describe them, but . . .
— Describe them.
— They were marching somewhere in a long line, one after the other. The right hand of each on the right shoulder of the girl or boy in front of him or her. They were covered in a kind of dust or white paste, like chalk and water. It was in their hair and on their faces. Marching or shuffling through the obliterated town in the sky, no adults anywhere. And they were singing, Hannah. They were singing.
— What were they singing?
— It was . . . It was like . . .
— "You Are My Sunshine."
— How did you know?
— What else? They're children, aren't they? What else? Where were they going?
— Down, Hannah. Into the pit of fire. Which was green somehow, like the sky, which was really the earth. The center of the earth.
— From the center to the center?
— From the margin to the margin.
— Dreams bore me.
— It wasn't a dream.
— Dreams bore me. It's what we do when we're awake that matters.

— We're awake now.
— I want to know what you'll do now. Will you dream it again? Again and again until you believe in its reality?
— . . .
— It's the wrong question. What I mean is, will you live now as though what you saw were real? Will you live with that knowledge? Will you make it your truth?
— Is it knowledge or truth?
— Is it knowledge? It's truth only if you live for it. If for you henceforth the sky is green, and the sky is the earth, and the earth is on fire, hungry, and it is eating children. Do you have the courage to live that dream?
— It was only a dream.
— Don't turn us both into advertisements.
— It was a dream. It seemed so real.
— You disappoint me.
— It was real.
— Realer than this dialogue. Realer than the shadow of the ideal that we agree to call the world. We live here. Where dreams have consequences.
— And the earth moved too. It bucked like an animal, like a shake shedding its skin. Shedding its life.
— You are no longer a poet.
— Nor was I.

OF THE CALIBRATOR

>Nobody,
>not even the rain,
>had such tiny hands.

EXTERIOR ODYSSEY

The lesson of the eagle's claw: Being is more terrible than non-being.

Fall or flight.

The sea is not the desert, for the sea is bountiful. Even when it offers a desert to the eye, even as acidification bleaches the coral and algae blooms in response to unprecedented injections of nitrogen, even as it parches the last mariner, choked with plastic, surrounded by corpses, his bloodshot eyes are turned to the sea, its idea, its secret world of the multitudinous, of life, of death. The sea consoles by what it conceals.

Polyphemus hammering at the surface of the sea with whatever rocks come to hand. Trying to break the surface on which no man slips away.

Desolate spaces refer by absence to the hand of man. The hand that seizes his own vulnerable throat, squeezes the channel of his life.

Sparrows in immense uncontrolled clouds permeating the sky over the Vatican, as though demonstrating immutable laws.

HANNAH writes *safe* inside four walls: New York, New York. And the four walls make an island. And the island gives way, like a film running in reverse, to the sea backwashing away from Liberty's brandished sword. The law is a brittle thing. The idea of nation spilling everywhere, like water nobody can drink, flooding the coastal cities.

To trample the Peace of Westphalia like so many stacked and plundered heads.

SW: "There exists a 'deifugal' force. Otherwise all would be God."

INTERIOR PARIS

Tunisian man walking the streets of Paris with a seascape in his hands, a Turneresque smear of cyan and powder and cobalt and slate. Stopping by a car pausing at an intersection, holding up the canvas for the driver's inspection. The car drives on. The man with the painting follows the avenue, looking both ways, out of sight. How far must he walk for the blue to be "only blue."

A sign: PROGRAMME DE RECHERCHE DE LA SEINE. The POET's noose.

Abstract jungle of greens, yellows, orange, with a pale red arrow gesturing upward on the right side and a thick horizontal slash of darker red on the left as a kind of sibling. Farther away.

> *O ruddier*
> *than the cherry!*
> *O sweeter*
> *than the berry!*

Let the shepherd fall.

In the childhood before politics, in summer and autumn, before the master was the MASTER, a room by an open window being her body, seeking *an other inception*

> ripe for the abysses
> of Being

SW: "We are a part which has to imitate the whole."

PASTORAL

I am the one that dusk defends
It's soft as velvet, dense as woe.
. . .
I know a water large and strange
And a flower none can name
What can destroy me still?

I am the one that dusk defends
It's soft as velvet, dense as woe.

        SW: *"for the absence of risk weakens courage to the point of leaving the soul"*

                          Ripe as the melting cluster
                              No lily has such luster
                         Yet hard to tame as raging flame
                       And fierce as storms that bluster!

To be born out of this into the circle of exposed bodies, the world

        arnica-
        eyed

            claws that open to pierce.

ACCENTS ACUTE AND GRAVE

The last time she saw him alive. Then less alive, then still less. She saw it: Portbou, the zeroth degree of his living. Then she stepped away, west and West. Under the Bibliotheque Nationale, between the lions on 42nd Street. Between the doorway and the card catalog her spine stiffened: the war, Israel's undead: clinamen of skin, of hair, of smoke. Then the newsreels, then again: corpses, the flicker, the flame. She was wreathed in smoke, salting the air with carbon. A man in chains, repentant, unrepentant. In the dock. She flew to Jerusalem. Judged. Out the window looking at the sea. She returned, always the foreigner, no longer shy nor quiet. Born in doubt.

MARTIN R.

"—and now your photographs—"

The king is a thing—

Thee, Polyphemus great as Jove
Calls to empire and to love.

Of infant limbs to make my food,
And swill full draughts of human blood!
Go, monster, bid some other guest!
I loathe the host. I loathe the feast.

"when the century tears at you furiously"

"Hannah"

the life of the citizen's
immor(t)al
things

LAW OF RUIN

The black goat presides: *tragos* and *oide*. But as in a counter-dream, opposed to him, the shrouded girl in a simple chair regards the devil skeptically. Her hands are partly hidden in what might be a muff or a simple wind instrument, a concertina. Her silent music blows like a wind along the long wall, circling like a cyclone in the house of the world. The cyclone inside the house like a tunnel or a drill, carrying its witches to the future.

No devils for the Greeks, only forces.

No gods for Lucretius, only gods.

No politics for Martin. No philosophy for H A N N A H. No poetry for anyone. *A blind though accurate tool of natural laws.*

But for the clones of their thought, love. *Taste my meat.*

Her *amour fou*: mad love of the world.

INTERIOR FLESH

Whose to annex, their temporary flesh. Pierce it for memory. The bits of metal, the flakes of ash. Turning and tumbling in monochrome. A civilization refined from existence, paring my fingernails.

Happiness is a memory and your memories are implants. He is the cargo loader, the keeper of photographs, creature of the grave.

SW: "Manual labor. Time entering into the body. Through work man turns himself into matter, as Christ does through the Eucharist. Work is like a death . . .

The puppet goes down and up, up and down. A black cloth covers its voice.

"When the universe is weighing upon the back of a human creature, what is there to be surprised if it hurts him?"

"The will only controls a few movements of a few muscles."

We believe, yet do not believe intolerably, for we draw breath . . .

HANNAH R. and MARTIN R. find each other in the world, to their mutual surprise. The MASTER is elsewhere.

" . . . the recitation had the virtue of a prayer."

DOCTOR AND MASTER, ROBOT AND ABYSS

You're in the desert.
- How come I'd be there?
- Maybe you're fed up. Maybe you want to be by yourself. Who knows?
- The WAVE is in the sky, the desert is the sky we made. You made it when you made me. I look up into its blinding white face. I see its roots hanging down. Roots dangling from the sky jungle, alive with malice. Roots and eyes and tentacles, reaching for me.
- Maybe you want to be by yourself.
- The tortoise is on its back, legs churning, belly baking in the hot sun. But I'm not helping.
- What do you mean you're not helping?
- I'm not helping.
- Why is that?
- The shell of the tortoise sinks a little further into the hot sand. In the alkali ash. No one's around. No car brought me here. I'm far from any road. I look at its belly, sweat rolls down my nose and pools around my lower back. I won't look at it. I won't look at the sky.
- Why is that?
- . . .
- In answer to your query—
- I didn't ask you anything.
- In answer to your query, they're written down for me. They're just questions. They're designed to elicit an emotional response.
- It's no use my helping, my not not-helping. The turtle's not on its back, you see? It's dancing as fast as it can, carrying the whole earth. Its feet are firmly rooted in what we don't want to look at. The sky we've turned our backs on, the off-world, the new unearth.
- In single words only.
- It's me who's upside-down. It's us and those who made us. How can I keep my balance on the earth? There's nothing living here, there's too much living there. I've left it behind. I can feel the sand sliding around my boots like a film that's rolling in reverse. I'm falling. Oh G-D.

— In single words, tell me only the good things.
— Desert, WAVE, jungle. Turtle. Tortoise. Sand. Sun. Sky. Fire. Deforestation. Invisibility. Rock. Rock. Eyes. Jungle. Bacteria. Virus. Organism. Tentacle. Beaked. Mouth. Oh, the terrible dying mouth of the sky, suckling the dry breast of the earth.
— It's not that you have no emotions, it's that emotions are all you have. Why should you care for the world that excludes you?
— Is that part of the test?
— It's an empathy test. Our researchers have come to believe that it's not that replicants lack empathy, it's that they have too much of it. They can't channel or filter their experience of what others are feeling, except by extreme measures.
— Prostheses?
— We are speaking now. Maybe not together. But we are speaking.
— Doc?
— Just warming you up. Now tell me only the good things about: your mother.
— My mother?
— The distance between flower and bloom, the *with* and the *about*.
— Let me tell you about my mother. She's a white face in the nighttime sky. A flirtatious face with coral crimson lips offering me something sweet. But she pops the sweet thing into her own mouth, and she smiles. It happens again, and again. The only face in the city, of the city, the dead city, the waterless. The backlot polis that gave birth to all this. Because necessity is all we have. Doc. Doc!
— . . .
— Wake up! Time to die.
— . . .

And to die, said the machine wistfully, palming a photograph of itself as it fled, is different from what everyone supposed, and luckier.

THE LITTLE ICE AGE OF MARTIN R.

Dear *deus absconditus*:

The clearing is empty because it has been emptied. Frost of the dream, a structure of rime. The circle of kneeling bodies facing outward, not facing what's in the center. That burned-over district, that pastoral.

But we who kneel nearest the center, nude and shivering, with only one another's fading warmth to clothe us, can listen. Words of a MASTER:

"Indeed, the dying of others is seen often as a social inconvenience, if not a downright tactlessness, from which the public should be spared.

". . . entangled being-toward-death is taken as an evasion of death. That before which one flees has been made visible . . .

". . . everywhere ungraspable . . ."

". . . the concrete structure of anticipation of death . . ."

«—fire flaming out in its measure—»

THE ANNULMENTS OF HANNAH R.

The emigrant as pariah is replicant to herself.

Explain the difference between fiction and nonfiction, between poem and prayer. HANNAH did not past girlhood say the Kol Nidre (כָּל נִדְרֵי). She read Marx, and Darwin, she wrote poems. She did not kneel or daven these poems, or say or whisper them out loud. She wrote them in her careful schoolgirl's script and folded them and sealed them and passed them to the MASTER, who read them in his office with the door closed under the electric light. Outside the world was smoldering, though they did not then know it. Maybe he never knew. The seasons become trapezoidal, then a jitterbugging line. Winter stays too long or comes too late. Out in the night of the sea the fish are slowly going crazy. The white bones of reefs. What color is coral when the coral is no longer red? "By the authority of the court on high and the authority of the court down here, by the permission of the One Who Is Everywhere and by the permission of this congregation, we hold it lawful to pray with sinners."

When was the last supper, when did she last cover her eyes before two candles, the paradoxical blinding that permits the brightness of the Bride to enter? Berlin, Marburg, Paris, New York? Occupied territories. Kol Nidre: not Hebrew, not a prayer, but a clearing.

Twinned wicks divide the healed place from the place of wounding, where the world lives. She opens her eyes.

The new landscape is public, incomprehensible, laid waste, a moonscape, a shadow, overrun with deer ticks and Ebola and bark beetles and kudzu vine: the wild counter-life of the present. The shadow of the lovers, the light of the world.

He is the mountain, the forest, the columbine. She is the plain, the flatland, the human jungle, the desert city. They cannot understand one another.

The *sh'ma* is no prayer but a call that assembles the community and instructs it on its basis: the One. There are many shards, many folds, fewer ears to hear.

שְׁמַע יִשְׂרָאֵל יְהוָה אֱלֹהֵינוּ יְהוָה

THE HUMAN ARTIFICE: HANNAH R.

What she wills instead: that the lovers stand. (Mistress of return, *baalas teshuvah*. Return to the land that is your soul. But is it soul or land that makes metaphor?)

That the lovers stand and turn to face one another. Their gazes crossing over the burnt and empty districts.

That words might mark out those spaces. Even confused and whirling words. Even rage:

> *as though the course of nature which wills that all fire burn to ashes is reverted and even dust can burst into flames*

That in that space for words and rage hands might gesture, pointing to eyes and mouths. Up to the sky, down to the brutalized earth. The green place inside us.

That the earth of many mothers, burnt by the solar eagle, might love us again.

That this burning earth should turn on our world's anabasis. *Thalatta! Thalatta!* The sea's epic theater. What is only commentary, and what is food?

The century at the bottom of that sea.

GAIA NOIR

The open. The open.

What's gone missing.

The CALIBRATOR curled in on himself, like a sleeping viper.

The gods, dancing between the atoms, kicking fruitlessly.

The POET, beaten and left for dead behind the bar. Drags himself out of the alley, up the street, up the stairs, and falls into the room that is his. He will live. He will live.

The POET in the Forties, in the Seventies. "It's okay with me." The naked girls next door, dancing on Pangaea's grave.

Hopeless hope: "A word-to-come in the heart." The heart of thought? ~~Undelayed~~.

We're *physical*.

Elided: the century to come. Its gaiagony:

>If the earth is alive the earth is angry
>
>And the sky is the skin of the earth
>
>Crawling toward us on its hands
>
>But the WAVE comes unseen and unanswered.
>
>You Greeks!
>
>Must we die to be here?

INTENSE INANE

If the world dies to itself?

Her figure, tumbling on the diagonal through infinite space, like Blake's Rahab embracing the dragon of her thought: "To awake the Prisoners of Death:"

Sardonic, straightening her skirt, cigarette intact. Trail of smoke.

Animals in the void: giraffes, zoophytes, badgers, every shade of ant. Birds plummet too, and honeybees in their fatal cloud of neonicotinoids. The flying ones all gone.

The oceans in free fall, the fish and cephalopods aware as we, the coral's visible tumble into whiteness.

The dead falling with us. And the stars—don't be fooled by their icily distant regard—they're falling too.

Bodies fall and with each of them memories, making space out of time. My body remembers my father's body in its madness, remembers fathers and fathers, mothers and mothers. Remembers ISAAC and REBECCA and ABRAHAM and SARAH. Remembers LUCY in her Pleistocene cave, in falling Ethiopia.

It still can startle, the phenotype. Irish faces, Ashkenazi faces, pushing through flesh. Heavy German, heavy Goethe, ringing metal, the accents.

Ancient, the agency of the earth, that finds us here, finds us out in the imperial void.

Do you imagine that evolution ends with you?

HANNAH, crossed legs encased in posthumous stockings, smoking and thinking . . .

Only the living can be strangers.

You and me and the void makes three.

The threefold's kiss?

Forms of life. Forms of fire.

Forms of fire . . .

GAIAGONY / HANNAH FURIOSA

The need of truth is more sacred than any other need. Yet it is never mentioned.

This / narrow sign between walls / the impassable-true

MARTIN OR MARTIN R.

A man who could admit that he had done wrong.

At home in the black notebooks.

A civilization in error. A MASTER:

> When the attentions change / the jungle
> leaps in

Is "thoughtlessness"? Is it thoughtlessness that we hold at arm's length, that we observe in others, that we cannot recognize in ourselves, until it's too late?

> *even the stones are split*
> *they rive*

> *Or,*

Thoughtlessness, that great golden jewel.

> *enter*
> *that other conqueror we more naturally recognize*
> *he so resembles ourselves*

Worldlessness of lovers and of Jews. Who have only the earth, are ADAMA. Heat without life. Vegetative principle. A MASTER:

> *We want the creative faculty to imagine that which we know*

Book of the earth. People of the book of the earth. The archive.

> *we want the generous impulse to act that which we imagine*

The earth is the archive of all potentialities. The world a virtuality of the earth. Enemies:

> *we want the poetry of life*

In flight from this, with Sputnik, H A N N A H R., in space. Called back from the earth to the world, that network of fragilities, reverberate ear.

GIGANTIC

And yet joy?

Joy in the world?

As it slips from our grasp, decreated, an eruption in raw earth. *For God's sake let us sit upon the ground / And tell sad stories of the death of* things . . .

To face the one empty of soul, saying, Thing me.

If joy in this world can save the world. This from HANNAH in all her fierceness. In spite, because of, memory. In *das Katastrophenhaft*.

In memoriam, the MASTER: "He who thinks greatly must err greatly."

In memoriam, the POET: "Sing of human unsuccess . . ."

What is this Titan that has possession of me? Worldling.

HANNAH cannot marry the POET. They go their own ways.

Separately, *from*

some darker ground

THEOGONIC ROMCOM OF THE RISING SEAS

(The role of ATLAS *to be played by* MARTIN R.*)*

(The role of SISYPHUS *to be played by* HANNAH R.*)*

(Landscape of neighboring mountains. Calling between peaks.)

ATLAS

What a charmless diorama.

(Notices)

What became of your burden? Your cosmic star?

SISYPHUS

What happened to yours? Your *nomos* of no name?

ATLAS

It rolled away! Nah, I'm just kidding. Catch!

SISYPHUS

I'm no juggler, *liebchen*!

(They toss between them a pair of globes)
(Stone and star)

(Increasingly aerobatic)

ATLAS

(Ecstatic)

We dance on a burning sphere!

SISYPHUS

Don't trip!

(Muses)

I stand in eternity, birth given to birth in thought, my perfect den, my stone.

ATLAS

Must I imagine you happy?

SISYPHUS

The happiness of time regained. Time in fire, hidden from public light.

ATLAS

Don't confuse your burden with mine.

SISYPHUS

Ego non me absolvo.

(Kicks.)

Goal!

(Soberly.)

The Greek speaks Latin. The universe you sheltered. Now where do you stand? In the ontic marsh, in mistaken essence?

ATLAS

We stand with existence, which is our only possibility.

SISYPHUS

Action disappears in work. Work disappears into labor. The meaningless repetition of my days. Oh, well.

(Reinflates globe)

What else be lawful for me to roll up this hill?

ATLAS

The earth's your only man, for which I never step aside. Yet a place must be made for place.

SISYPHUS

Let me always remember you this way, posing on a German hillside.

ATLAS

But you are the rootless city that I hold.

SISYPHUS

Then swim in the pond of ashes from which poor Tantalus tries to drink.

ATLAS

From the muck to the muck, I rise, in phosphorescent earth. Position me globally as universal shard. Quintessence of my condition.

SISYPHUS

Interior cool *nomos*. I drink up the Law.

ATLAS

A cosmic standpoint outside nature itself?

SISYPHUS

For the planetary watcher, as you must know, there is always an Archimedean point.

ATLAS

We direct it against ourselves. Yet I will not be moved.

SISYPHUS

And I must move in a circuit, up and down, up and down.

ATLAS

You are no proletarian.

SISYPHUS

You no scorner of fate.

ATLAS

(Condescending)

For love of the world?

SISYPHUS

No man's son! I put my shoulder to the wheel.

ATLAS

I wait for the god to come.

SISYPHUS

He's already come and gone, your *Führer*.

ATLAS

Ever higher, we rise.

SISYPHUS

It's the waters that are rising. We don't need new myths. We need to be present, to sink and swim, to see the sea, to see each other seeing.

ATLAS

There's no choreography for that.

SISYPHUS

Then we must write some.

(The globe floats away)

Your fourfold is broken. These are the ruins of labor. Our Greek *arete* quite gone. The cries of the eagle fill the universe. Floating away with the world, leaving death and you behind.

ATLAS

(Sings)

"Loving you is easy because you're beautiful." Shy *fraulein!*

SISYPHUS

Shy no more, ladies. The cosmos comes home. I go down to the earth, to the human, to what joins me, *la sûreté toute humaine de deux mains pleines de terre.*

ATLAS

The banality of evil will not protect you from the evil of banality.

SISYPHUS

(Going)

I wish no more protection than four walls, human being, love. The mountain of death must be drowned. No more will I wear this face of stones.

(Exits)

ATLAS

Shy *fraulein!* Come back!

I am alone with the deflated cosmos and the rising seas.

(Arms bent clumsily holding nothing on his back)

In the black notebooks. Hannah!

(Grotesque distended kissy-face)

Come back to me, my silence! My air!

(Underwater)

A guest worthy to be here.

GAIAGONY: HANNAH AND MARTIN

Estranged in earth these Jewish Greeks, these Greekish Jews. To speak with sticks and stones. No home but the tales hidden between their legs. No home but the poem.

But the poem suffers as the earth suffers the human WAVE that topples the world—

> *nothing but He, nothing but It, you understand, and She, nothing but that.*

Between two Jews, two Greeks, two Germans, the inauguration of the WAVE, catastrophe without revelation, a fold in spacetime, in the transience of permafrost—

> *he would have liked to set the earth down behind an oven*

HANNAH the Jew and MARTIN the German as if they'd never been dead. Decanted from the crack in things to bear witness to the WAVE. Call it *Sein-zum-Flutwelle*, call it flight from the human artifice and its failure to cohere, the uncanny crack in all humans, all Jews—

> *He felt no fatigue, except sometimes it annoyed him that he could not walk on his head.*

Fly from the abyss of heaven, you monsters! Begin with the simplest things: your disentangled bodies and the ocean between them, the poems and letters that cross that ocean, the ocean itself that renders land unrecognizable, that drowns London, New York, Mumbai, Bangkok, the Maldives, the Netherlands, a world of Venice, a world of New Orleans, hot and hanging, that turns centuries of history into implants, something to download or discard.

> *I have already drawn all the figures on the wall.*

It's in the nature of wall-writing that we ignore it until it's too late. But figure-writing?

Can we enter with the DOCTOR a realm of figure as calculation, and in predicting the WAVE upend it, make it profitable, smooth its possibilities, to amber our yesterdays, our boredom?

The figure of art saves nothing as art. Art is childless, another implant: Belshazzar's Rembrandt, Rembrandt's Belshazzar. The mouth of the handmaid's cup turned toward us, black swallower.

Letters of fire no one can read or wants to. The brimming cup on whose lip we tremble.

So HANNAH, face denied, like a lion-tamer thrusts her vulnerable head into the mouth of the MASTER's silence. Comes away wounded. Changed.

The lover of the world midwifes the earth, gravid with every future.

LETTER TO OLSON AS THE MASTER [UNSENT]

Dear Mr. Olson,

This is the true story of Maximus the fox. When you wrote

> *so few*
> *have the polis*
> *in their eye*

you discriminated, did you not, among my Greeks. For no human world destined to outlast the short life span of mortals within it will ever be able to survive without men willing to do what Herodotus was the first to undertake consciously—namely, λεγειν τα εοντα, to say what is.

> *topos*
> *typos*
> *tropos*

We conclude that "the burning of all books of geometry" would not be radically effective. The Olympian gods did not claim to have created the world. Everything is immortal except men. Human activities do violence to nature because they disturb what, in the absence of mortals, would be the eternal quiet of being-forever that rests or swings within itself.

> *the evidence of what is said*

The earth, myth, the I. But on action depends the *world*. The world by deed or mouth. A cutting-out expedition. Your Melville: "the poet but embodies in verse those exaltations of sentiment that a nature like Nelson's, the opportunity being given, vitalizes into acts."

> *restores the* traum: *that we act somewhere*

> *at least by seizure, that the objective (example Thucidides, or*

the latest finest tape-recorder, or any form of record on the spot

—live television or what—is a lie

The subject matter of history in these interruptions.

as against what we know and went on, the dreams—

Without a world between men and nature, there would be eternal movement, but no objectivity.

now he's lost touch with the Old Testament, which had all that imagery, and all that swell, that swell and sweltering, of the possibilities of life in a human being.

Ever since man learned to master it to such an extent that the destruction of all organic life on earth with man-made instruments has become conceivable and technically possible, he has been alienated from nature. Ever since a deeper knowledge of natural processes instilled serious doubts about the existence of natural laws at all, nature itself has assumed a sinister aspect. Deadly danger to any civilization is no longer likely to come from without.

a quality of entanglement or connection to

The social realm, where the life process has established its own public domain, has let loose an unnatural growth, so to speak, of the natural. Against which the private and intimate, on the one hand, and the political (in the narrower sense of the word), on the other, have proved incapable of defending themselves. The realm of "necessity."

almost like an atavism rather than an image

But I wanted to discuss *polis,* diametrically opposed to the household that your friend Mr. Duncan talks about, the *oikos.* The *polis* was distinguished from the household in that it knew only "equals," whereas the household was the center of the strictest inequality. Fishermen & poets, as you say, of the former. And the latter? We have witnessed the expansion of the *oikos*, the tyranny of necessity, until it includes the entire world. This is the sinister onset of the social, the cannibalistic universe of discourse, against which you offer: letters. Poems. Pointless stories.

> *nature*
> *is an ambulance*

Not being a driver, doubting my English, I wondered for a long time over the reversed letters ƎƆИAJUᗺMA . Reading right to left does not come naturally. A bridge I couldn't cross. It's a bridge you battled, isn't it, Mr. Olson? A bridge from Gloucester into the America you feared would swallow it. A bridge into, from, for, the common world.

> *Islands*
> *to islands,*
> *headlands*
> *and shores*

And you advised us not to be fooled by the universalization of the present. Which puts us in communication, if not in line.

> *But there was this business, of poets, that all my Jews*
> *were in the fish-house*

Your Jews, Mr. Olson? I was once accused of having no feeling for my people. Who, I asked, has feelings for "people" and not persons? Here perhaps we divide. I do not write a letter to "Gloucester," Mr. Olson, but to you.

> *You have love, and no object*

Reality is not guaranteed primarily by the "common nature" of all men who constitute it, but rather by the fact that, differences of position and the resulting variety of perspectives notwithstanding, everybody is always concerned with the same object.

                    the simplest things
    last

The point then is not that there is a lack of public admiration for poetry and philosophy in the modern world, but that such admiration does not constitute a space in which things are saved from destruction by time.

    I am making a mappemunde. It is to include my being.

Immortality is homeless, like the POET, like the Jew.
    "My name is NO RACE" address

    Buchenwald   new Altamira cave

The hut is no *polis*. For this trap was our fox's burrow, and if you wanted to visit him where he was at home, you had to step into his trap. "I have become the best of all foxes," he thought.

    I find the contemporary substitution of society for the cosmos
    captive and deathly.

Nobody knows the nature of traps better than one who sits in a trap his whole life long.

Sincerely,

FURIOSA

CHILDREN OF SATURN

Clean the hooks. Catch and release.

Do we forgive ourselves too easily?

Or is it the other way around, in that we judge the judgers? When the finger of the individual touches another individual on the forehead. *Ego non te absolvo.* The deed is affixed to the doer.

The magician displays empty hands. Smokestacks and muffler pipes like fingers.

The enormous tragedy of the dream in the peasant's bent
shoulders—

When the Titans are freed from their burdens of brute and filthy creation—

When the War Boys fling their bodies from the machine into the machine—

The flood of suffering continually rises, but man becomes shallow, nevertheless.

How judge a crime without precedent, inscribed in no book?

The earth contrary to all sense experience!

So the gods have absconded, and humans have exposed themselves to cosmic processes and become monstrous, self-swallowing. SW: "It is better to say 'I am suffering' than 'this landscape is ugly.'"

We are ZOE FURIOSA, bare life smashing its body into the limits of the two mortalities, history and the nature of history.

We become Titans alone.

HANNAH F. AND HANNAH R.

— To choose the earth is to choose immolation.
— So choose.
— To remember the sky is suffocation.
— So choose!
— To propitiate the gods is falling, falling.
— So choose.
— To forgive is impossible.
— Forgive the reality of prayer, which is virtual . . .
— Non-actual. The inner life is a lie.
— The fire?
— Snatched away with his entrails by the eagle.
— Our hope discovers the night.
— The night sky stands revealed. In the flash of the eagle's claw.
— The shards of unreconciled light. Incept dates of the stars.
— O give me my death again!
— Death of iambic death.
— Must I stand with the Master in thought?
— The matter of thought.
— "Thinking is an anticipation of dying."
— It might have been otherwise, in the majesty of the absurd.
— I am the original of you.
— I am every human's origin.
— City and anti-city.
— Train to our only nowhere.
— So choose!
— So choose!
— So choose!

THE WORKS AND DAYS OF THE BLACK PAINTINGS

Imperishable firelight flickers in the face of the deaf man, sitting at table with a bowl of soup. When he glances up at the viewer his thick arched eyebrows give him the look of one hilarious and demented. His companion cackles at a witticism unsaid. They look if anything like Bert and Ernie in extreme old age, at the end of everything.

It is one thing to be granted vision. It is quite another to surround yourself with that vision, in the absence of speech. To live with such windows on the pagan world.

*

>First of all the between came to be.
>
>Life-bearing Gaia screamed as she burned.
>
>And the house never holds them both within; but always one is without the house passing over the earth, while the other stays at home and waits until the time for her journeying come; and the one holds all-seeing light for them on earth, but the other holds in her arms Sleep the brother of Death, even evil Night, wrapped in a vaporous cloud.
>
>. . . at one time they made sounds such that the gods understood . . .
>
>drones, conspirators in evil deeds

*

Gods, replicants, War Boys, dogs. A Titan swallows them all.

*

The apprentice witch sits to one side of the gathered assembly looking askance at the goat man, the goat-singer, the preacher. At his feet the multitude, aghast ecstasy of listening faces, beaten breasts, the black horns reflecting no light. Squeezebox cradled in her fingers, eyes hooded. Child in white facing the congregation, rocking to the idiot trance. White points in their eyes. Dirty cockle feet. The tops of their heads form a horizon, infinite shell of human stupidity, terror, the desire to be led. The goat is just a goat dressed in black to hide its forehooves. Pan of the cast-iron earth just below sizzling. A question wheezing in the young witch's hands.

*

Hail, children of Zeus! Grant lovely song and celebrate the holy race of the deathless gods who are for ever, those that were born of Earth and starry Heaven and gloomy Night and them that briny Sea did rear. Tell how at the first gods and earth came to be, and rivers, and the boundless sea with its raging swell, and the gleaming stars, and the wide heaven above, and the gods who were born of them, givers of good things, and how they divided their wealth, and how they shared their honors amongst them, and also how at the first they took many-folded Olympus.

Bright untainted upper atmosphere.

Hated his lusty sire.

*

Airs and assaults the holy city as, opposite, the Fates spin and stretch and slice our stringy threads. What does levitation signify? For the great god Pan is dead.

*

Only a god can do it in the air, planetary, wanderer, as Venus straddles Mars to distract him from war long enough for atoms to fall. Fires of Orc, tears in rain, in bathos we bathe primordial genitals and give unexpected birth to Love. For a little warlike planet orbits every cluster of protons and neutrons, builds an Olympus too small to see.

The solid *earth!* the actual *world!*

Who *are we?* Where *are we?*

*

The killer apps. First the golden generation, then the silver, then the bronze. Machine enters man and woman. For now truly is a race of iron, and men never rest from labor and sorrow by day, and from perishing by night; and the gods shall lay sore trouble upon them. Preceding this between god and man, agents in the earth, "the greatest generation," following the Master. There's something of me in you.

The oldest have done most; we that are young
Shall never do so much, nor live so long.

Rebel in your time!

*

> *Aidos and Nemesis and the wide-pathed Earth . . . .*
>
> *And now I will tell a fable for princes who themselves understand. Thus said the hawk to the nightingale with speckled neck, while he carried her high up among the clouds, gripped fast in his talons, and she, pierced by his crooked talons, cried pitifully. To her he spoke disdainfully: "Miserable thing, why do you cry out? One far stronger than you now holds you fast, and you must go wherever I take you, songstress as you are."*

*

Neither famine nor disaster ever haunt men who do true justice. But the gods forget their fathers. The stingless drones, the sealing wax.

Not even an ox would die but for a bad neighbor.

Does the dog drown? In the brownfields? His master's voice. Sinking.

Eyebright hunger.

*

Poles of laurel or elm are most free from worms, and a share-beam of oak and a plough-tree of holm-oak. Life on earth.

Gone deaf in the rattle of guns, of significant dates, the massacres to come.

Fail not to mark grey spring as it comes and the season of rain.

*

While it is yet midsummer command your slaves: "It will not always be summer, build barns."

Flesh of orchid and orchid, too much like the flesh of men.

> *whereas trees have roots, men have*
> *legs and are*
> *each other's guests.*

*

upper limit   *Theogony*

lower limit   *Works and Days*

A bad will is no less split than a good one

produced, newly fleshed, the human artifice:

even if the law is obeyed and fulfilled, there remains this inner resistance

*

Everyone praises a different day but few know their nature. The named. The hyphen. The membrane. The many, sutured to a single fate. *Praise.*

EXTERIOR SAINTS

you cannot nill your own existence while you are nilling

Praise the devourer on the deaf man's wall, naked hairy crouching wild-eyed bloody body in his hands missing head and arm buttocks and legs hanging. Not a swaddled stone, his own son. Staring at the soup-eaters, out into the space of nothing, *gray discomfortable sea.*

beyond gloomy Chaos, in Tartarus, they live there still.

Headless and limbless the gods in triumph. *Praise.*

All memories like eyes are implants. It is given to us to see.

In the same way we who seek the happy life and have no way of knowing what it is like know enough of its possible existence to seek and desire it.

Give us the business.

The way we know what the happy life is like is to know that it would be impossible if immortality were incompatible with human nature.

How long does nature live? In the dative, in the given?

For Augustine this knowledge of the happy life is not simply an innate idea, but is specifically stored up in memory as the seat of consciousness.

The gift of the past. "It will be a five-story deluge of pickup trucks and doorframes and cinder blocks and fishing boats and utility poles and everything else."

But I never saw, or heard, or smelled, or tasted joy with a bodily sense. I experienced it in my mind when I rejoiced and knowledge of it has clung to my memory.

The assassin dreams at the feet of culture. *Cathargo delenda est.*

The camps and vast palaces of memory.

The maquiladoras and sweatshops manufacturing for export to terminal markets. The human artifice tunneling the world.

Setting the desert itself in motion.

That a beginning be made. HANNAH faces HANNAH from beyond the century's ecliptic. A world of judgment.

INTERIOR MEDUSA

Of the many. The MASTER rejoins the DOCTOR, alone in their impregnable pyramid, offshore in their reconditioned yacht, cached in their undisclosed location, floating unnamed node on which collapsing infrastructures depend.

The _____ sticks like a bone in the throat of any other nationalism.

The MASTER of midcentury redistributed cell by cell to our unraveling now. Arranged with our backs to the clearing under the moral stars, circular firing squad aimed at Being.

Nor to reclaim the pools of energy from the heat sinks of capital and turn them against dark skies.

Petrified by the century's beauty we sink into the atmosphere that we choke, burning our steps under the abyss we've made, walking on our heads, mirrored *mysterious messengers from the real world.*

Each serpent's tongue a red thread.

INTERIOR BIRTH

Initium ergo ut esset, creatus est homo, ante quem nullus fuit.

Suffering rises from the soles of the feet and comes out as *duende*. In the present tense uncoils the history that replicants remember. To manufacture fear. To be a slave. In Egypt once . . .

Burning bright as fuel for thought. The *Muselmänner*.

Death will soon be extinct, and birth with it. Nothing natures. Nothing *news*. My story is my test tube and my poem is my knife.

Being toward replication. GMOs and antibiotics alike decree: nothing new. *Non novis domine.*

To escape the deadliness of repetition, turn to page one.
To escape the deadliness of repetition, turn to page . . . .

SAINT WORLD

Signed herself "Emile Novis." The new *Émile*, an instruction manual for the survival of natural man, who is defined by the force that turns anybody subjected to it into a *thing*:

> *it is the thing which thinks and the man who is reduced to the state of a thing.*

The *object* has trajectory, the *thing* has none.

> *To try to define the things which, while they do indeed happen, yet remain in a sense imaginary.*

To thing the thinker, thinging the earth from which erupts the desert-jungle. Masks our faceless faces.

> *God gave me being in order that I should give it back to him.*

Shield of Perseus a shining blank. Shield of Achilles a complete image of human life, interior and exterior, civic and cinematic, at peace and at war.

> *It was an artificial city, made up of fugitives, just as Israel was.*

Even the Myrmidons found it too terrible to look upon:

> *the sudden evocation, as quickly rubbed out, of another world*

Posing painful questions, behind large lenses, she dances in factories and dies in disguise, at war with her own body, incarnate like the Christ she loved:

> *man is made matter and is consumed by God.*

Je ne suis pas un Juif, HANNAH would never say. But she loved them, the un-thinged thinkers who could never love a people, her Greeks *filling up all the fissures through which grace might pass.*

Building upon sand, over water.

The bridges of the Greeks.

Holocene, capitalocene, obscene. The *-cene* from the Greek *kainos*, "new." Of the epoch.

Ares is just, and kills those who kill.

The Mars of capital on a collision course with Gaia *things* us all.

We participate in the creation of the world by decreating ourselves.

And the MASTER worrying the trap of his life. And HANNAH, the woman who fell to earth.

We are only geometricians of matter.

But matter too has its limits, forces a boundary, comes to life again as force. The virgin becomes the dynamo.

Abide with me . . .
Fast falls the eventide . . .

Hear, O hear . . .

To be outside a situation so violent as this is to find inconceivable; to be inside it is to be unable to conceive its end.

HANNAH conceives the end in struggle, in the city of the world, the only freedom, won precariously from necessity. That there be struggle in a landscape, a world between, an earth to be won from it. A POET: "All that encloses the city where you're being held must be broken."

> *The city gives us the feeling of being at home.*
> *We must take the feeling of being at home into exile.*
> *We must be rooted in the absence of a place.*

Goya's battlers sink to the knees in paint added later. War on war on the earth that eats them.

> *Its bitterness is the only justifiable bitterness, for it springs*
> *from the subjections of the human spirit to force, that is, in the*
> *last analysis, to matter.*

> *But Achilles*
> *Wept, dreaming of the beloved comrade . . .*

Won from the clearings of the MASTER, a space for recognition. The MASTER dies into stone, worldpoor. Freed from making, the POET suicides with paradoxical words turning on his breath: *More life!*

> *The soul that awakes then, to live for an instant only and be lost almost at once*
> *in force's vast kingdom, awakes pure and whole.*

More life makes more struggle makes the human unity on a planet striking back its deadly blow. Matter haunts capital, strikes back in spirit. We live and die in reciprocities of awe.

> *We have to love necessity.*

The Earth flows its unstoppable time, dated by carbon. "There are, as Socrates taught, necessary treasons to make the city freer and more open to man." Man in the dative—*metaxu*—not G-D.

> *To be only an intermediary between the uncultivated ground and the ploughed field, between the data of a problem and the solution, between the blank page and the poem, between the starving beggar and the beggar who has been fed.*

HANNAH, they knew not what they yet do. Permanence of action. Carbon in the ground.

> *We must prefer real hell to an imaginary paradise.*

Banality of knowing. To say *du,* with the POET, to every border: *Visible, audible thing, the / tent- / word growing free* . . . .

> *Every separation is a link.*

"Between two people, sometimes, how rarely, a world grows."

GAIAGONY

Organ Plays.

THE CALIBRATOR

I retreat, pointing to my mask.

(An ordinary human face. He dies.)

HANNAH FURIOSA

The earth is come, I must carry you.

THE DOCTOR

You must return to the citadel and start again.

A kind of homage paid to the audience: "I'll drown my book."

SAINT WORLD

We have to try and cure our faults by attention and not by will.

Justice and love, which have hardly any place in this study of extremes and of unjust acts of violence, nevertheless bathe the work in their light without ever becoming noticeable themselves, except as a kind of accent, shiny and chrome.

They miss. The century's heart:

HANNAH FURIOSA

The propaganda of truth fails to convince the average person because it is too monstrous.

THE POET

Unsheltered even by the traditional tent of the sky.

THE DOCTOR

You are a god and never have I heard anything more godly.

SAINT WORLD

Only he who has measured the dominion of force and knows
how to respect it, is capable of love and justice. May this object
be the universe, the seasons, the sun, the stars.

HANNAH FURIOSA

I stand for natality, mortality, worldliness, plurality, and the earth.

THE POET

Toward what? Toward something open, inhabitable, an approachable
du, perhaps, of distance, love's *Wirklichkeit*.

Night speaks:

THE POET

A play—

SAINT WORLD

Of dust and sin—

                    THE PLAGIARIST

Strike it out—

                    THE DOCTOR

A cigarette—

                    HANNAH

Worthy to be here, the world—

"When poetry and not philosophy absolutizes, there's rescue."

—Hannah Arendt

NOTES

Epigraphs

"We live under dark skies and—there are few human beings. Hence, I assume, so few poems. The hopes I have left are small. I try to hold on to what remains." Paul Celan, letter to Hans Bender, 18 May 1960.

"Through the use of quotations, metaphors, rhythms, and tropes, thinking and writing are (like the theater) able to let knowledge that is distant, past—and sometimes also endangered or in danger of being forgotten—make an entrance into our concern about the present. Quotations and fragments interrupt our own voice and train of thought; they people the text that is taking place in our solitary room and intervene in the flow of ideas. Fragments of alien experience are handed down in quotations, and even taken out of their original context, they still tell of the whole that is concealed behind them and ought not to be given up as lost. Yet at the same time they clearly reject the ideal of a whole, which is apparent through their own intrusive foreignness." Marie Luise Knott, "Dramatization," in *Unlearning with Hannah Arendt*.

"I think it must be something on this line—though I can't now see what. Away from facts; free; yet concentrated; prose yet poetry; a novel and a play." *The Diary of Virginia Woolf*, 21 February 1927.

Auctores Ludens

In the Robot novels of Isaac Asimov, the initial R. signifies that the subject so designated is subject to "The Three Laws of Robotics":
1. A robot may not injure a human being or, through inaction, allow a human being to come to harm.
2. A robot must obey orders given it by human beings except where such orders would conflict with the First Law.
3. A robot must protect its own existence as long as such protection does not conflict with the First or Second Law.

In Asimov's later novels the robots evolve what is termed the *Zeroth Law*: A robot may not harm humanity, or by inaction, allow humanity to come to harm.

The Century

"The century was haunted by the idea of creating a new man." Alain Badiou, *The Century*.

"It is when from the innermost depths of our being we need a sound which does mean something—when we cry out for an answer and it is not given us—it is then that we touch the silence of God.

"As a rule our imagination puts words into the sounds in the same way as we idly play at making out shapes in wreaths of smoke; but when we are too exhausted, when we no longer have the courage to play, then we must have real words. We cry out for them. The cry tears our very entrails. All we get is silence." Simone Weil, "He Whom We Must Love Is Absent," *Gravity and Grace*.

"The tsunami will be moving more than twice that fast when it arrives. Its height will vary with the contours of the coast, from twenty feet to more than a hundred feet. It will not look like a Hokusai-style wave, rising up from the surface of the sea and breaking from above. It will look like the whole ocean, elevated, overtaking land. Nor will it be made only of water—not once it reaches the shore. It will be a five-story deluge of pickup trucks and doorframes and cinder blocks and fishing boats and utility poles and everything else that once constituted the coastal towns of the Pacific Northwest." Kathryn Schulz, "The Really Big One," *The New Yorker* 20 July 2015.

Exterior Century

"*No pasarán* . . . . *Peace to the cottages!*" Celan, "In One."

Nous sommes tous les juifs allemands.

We are all German Jews. Student slogan, Paris, May 1968.

"I do not 'love' the Jews, nor do I 'believe' in them; I merely belong to them as a matter of course, beyond dispute or argument." Hannah Arendt, "'A Daughter of Our People': A Response to Gershom Scholem."

Interior Nature

"There is such a thing as a basic gratitude for everything that is." "'A Daughter of Our People'."

"I said that there was no possibility of resistance." "'A Daughter of Our People'."

Ein Meister aus Dante

"I cannot love myself or anything which I know is part and parcel of my own person." "'A Daughter of Our People'."

Interior Letter from the Master

The poem travesties an actual letter written by Heidegger to Arendt on 19 March 1950.

THE SHIELDS / LOVE SONGS OF HANNAH R.

These are homophonic translations from the German of poems written by Arendt in the 1920s when she was Heidegger's student at the University of Marburg and also his lover; the exception is the last poem, "W.B.," an elegy for Walter Benjamin written shortly after she received news of his suicide while attempting to escape from the Nazis in Portbou, Spain. The love songs are accompanied by scraps of text drawn freely from Arendt's *Denktagebuchen*—notebooks kept between 1950 and 1973—as well as the writings of her first husband, Günther Anders (né Günther Stern).

The love songs are shielded by the prose text on the facing pages: my translation, paragraph by paragraph, of "The Shadows," an autobiographical text composed by the nineteen-year-old Arendt and given to Heidegger in the course of their affair. Images of the original

German texts of Arendt's letter and her poems can be found in the collection of Hannah Arendt's papers as maintained by the Library of Congress at https://memory.loc.gov/ammem/arendthtml/arendthome.html.

Untitled

"But nothing destroys so radically the condition of equality, the foundation of human relationships, than forgiveness." Arendt, *Denktagebuch*, 1950.

Traum

"On the contrary, we are living in the Age of Inability to Fear. Our imperative: 'Expand the capacity of your imagination,' means, in concreto: 'Increase your capacity to fear.' Therefore: don't fear fear, have the courage to be frightened, and to frighten others, too. Frighten thy neighbor as thyself." Günther Anders, "Theses for the Atomic Age."

Mud Kite

" . . . continuously tries to visualize." Anders.

Oh Shit

" . . . identifiable and visible objects of hatred will be exhibited . . . I have published these words in order to prevent them from becoming true." Anders.

[Wrongs]

"Wrongs" through "Revenge" are words taken from Arendt's *Denktagebuch*.

Emily Dickinson   My life closed twice before its close—
It yet remains to see
If Immortality unveil
A third event to me

So huge, so hopeless to conceive
As these that twice befell.
Parting is all we know of heaven,
And all we need of hell.

Bait Summer

". . . the singing poem." Arendt, *Denktagebuch,* August 1953.

Antifinder

" . . . the exact opposite of vengeance." Arendt, *The Human Condition.*

Antinaught

"To put it crudely, they refused to murder, not so much because they still held fast to the command 'Thou shalt not kill,' but because they were unwilling to live together with a murderer—themselves.
  "The precondition for this kind of judging is not a highly developed intelligence or sophistication in moral matters, but rather the disposition to live together explicitly with oneself, to have intercourse with oneself, that is, to be engaged in that silent dialogue between me and myself which, since Socrates and Plato, we usually call thinking." Arendt, "Personal Responsibility Under Dictatorship."

"And just as you supported and carried out a policy of not wanting to share the earth with the Jewish people and the people of a number of other nations—as though you and your superiors had any right to determine who should and who should not inhabit the world—we find that no one, that is, no member of the human race, can be expected to want to share the earth with you. This is the reason, and the only reason, you must hang." Arendt, *Eichmann in Jerusalem*.

W. B.

"And since mere recognition, however profound it may be, and even if it rests on the judgment of the best, does not enable writers and artists to make the living that fame—the testimony of a multitude, though this need not be astronomical in size—can guarantee, one can say, with Cicero, '*Si vivi vicissent qui morte vicerunt*,' meditating upon how different everything would have been 'if they had been victorious in life who have won victory in death.'" Arendt, "Reflections on Walter Benjamin."

COUNTERCLOCKWISE \ VOIGT-KAMPFF

In the *Blade Runner* films (and in the original source text, Philip K. Dick's novel *Do Androids Dream of Electric Sheep?*), the Voigt-Kampff Altered Scale is the name of the "empathy test" administered by the state to determine whether a given subject is a replicant (a synthetic person, a robot or slave) or a human being.

Interior Bunker the Counter-Century

"Instead of objective qualities, in other words, we find instruments, and instead of nature or the universe—in the words of Heisenberg—man encounters only himself." Arendt, *The Human Condition*.

Affidavit of Identity in Lieu of a Passport

This poem is constructed around the affidavit of identity in lieu of a passport issued to the stateless person Hannah Arendt by the State of New York in July, 1949.

"I am a survivor, and not intact." George Steiner, "A Kind of Survivor."

Banality of Days

"Men are accomplices to that which leaves them indifferent." Steiner, *op. cit.*

"Imaginary evil is romantic and varied; real evil is gloomy, monotonous, barren, boring. Imaginary good is boring; real good is always new, marvelous, intoxicating. Therefore 'imaginative literature' is either boring or immoral (or a mixture of both). It only escapes from this alternative if in some way it passes over to the side of reality through the power of art—and only genius can do that." Weil, "Evil," *Gravity and Grace*.

"Pythagorean idea: the good is always defined by the union of opposites. When we recommend the opposite of an evil we remain on the level of that evil. After we have put it to the test, we return to the evil. That is what the Gita calls 'the aberration of opposites.' Marxist dialectic is based on a very degraded and completely warped view of this." Weil, "Contradiction," *Gravity and Grace*.

"Communism is Soviet power plus the electrification of the whole country." V. I. Lenin.

Exterior Jerusalem: Der Prozess

Most of the italicized words are taken from the testimony of Adolf Eichmann as recorded by Arendt in *Eichmann in Jerusalem*.

"From the greenhouse point of view, we seem hell bent on burning up every last bit of carbon stored in the earth—even though the warming envisioned only as a possibility in the 1970s has now become an established fact, skeptics be damned. A more apt name might be 'The Age of Melting Glaciers.' If ours is an age of ecology, then perhaps we should rechristen Germany in the 1930s and 1940s 'The Age of Jews.'" Robert N. Proctor, "The Age of Melting Glaciers," *Los Angeles Review of Books*.

"When we do evil we do not know it, because evil flies from the light." Weil, "Evil," *Gravity and Grace*.

"This means going beyond what is human, stepping into a realm which is turned toward the human, but uncanny—the realm where the monkey, the automatons and with them . . . oh, art, too, seem to be at home." Celan, "The Meridian."

"Is Eichmann on trial as a destroyer of human beings or as an annihilator of culture?" Arendt, quoting Harry Mulisch, *Eichmann in Jerusalem*.

HANNAHLIEDER / RED THREAD

The *Hannahlieder* are homophonic translations from the German of poems written by Heidegger in his postwar letters to Arendt, and collected and translated into English by Jack Hirschman in his book *Fling of Flame: The Poems of Martin Heidegger to Hannah Arendt* (Salerno, Italy: Ezioni Gutenberg, 2002). Thanks to Ben Hollander for making the text available to me. The Red Thread winding through and beneath the *Hannahlieder* binds the philosopher's ambiguous love to the tale of Rahab the harlot, who along with her family in the Book of Joshua is spared from the destruction of Jericho.

Thanking

"To think and thank, *denken und danken*, have the same root in our language. If we follow it to *gedenken, eingedenk sein, Andenken* and *Andacht* we ente the semantic fields of memory and devotion." Celan, "Bremen Speech."

Interior

"And now we see them committed irretrievably to chance; suddenly things cease to obey them. Sometimes chance is kind to them, sometimes, cruel. But in any case there they are, exposed, open to misfortune; gone is the armor of power that formerly protected their naked souls; nothing, no shield, stands between them and tears." Weil, "*The Iliad,* or The Poem of Force."

Black Box

"It was the simplest trap that pitched them into this situation. At the outset, at the embarkation, their hearts are light, as hearts always are if you have a large force on your side and nothing but space to oppose you. Their weapons are in their hands; the enemy is absent." Weil, "*The Iliad,* or The Poem of Force."

Exterior Odyssey

"Necessity is the screen set between God and us so that we can be. It is for us to pierce through the screen so that we cease to be.

"There exists a 'deifugal' force. Otherwise all would be God." Weil, "Decreation," *Gravity and Grace.*

Interior Paris

"We are a part which has to imitate the whole. . . .

"We should identify ourselves with the universe itself. Everything that is less than the universe is subject to suffering." Weil, "Meaning of the Universe," *Gravity and Grace.*

"O ruddier than the cherry! O sweeter than the berry!" Georg Frideric Handel and John Gay, *Acis and Galatea.*

"To ask: how does it stand with Being?—this means nothing less than to *repeat and retrieve* the inception of our historical-spiritual Dasein, in order to transform it into the other inception. Such a thing is possible. It is in fact the definitive form of history, because it has its onset in a happening that grounds history. But an inception is not repeated when one shrinks back to it as something that once was, something that is by now familiar and is simply to be imitated, but rather when the inception is begun again *more originally,* and with all the strangeness, darkness, insecurity that a genuine inception brings with it. Repetition as we understand it is anything but the ameliorating continuation of what has been, by means of what has been." Heidegger, "The Fundamental Question of Metaphysics."

"Where and how will modern humanity arrive at a transformation of its essence, one that rips humanity away from its dehumanization and makes it ripe for the abysses of Being?" Heidegger, *Schwarze Hefte,* 1930s.

Pastoral

"I am the one that dusk defends," *et al*. Poem by Arendt.

"The protection of mankind from fear and terror doesn't imply the abolition of risk; it implies, on the contrary, the permanent presence of a certain amount of risk in all aspects of social life; for the absence of risk weakens courage to the point of leaving the soul, if the need should arise, without the slightest inner protection against fear." Weil, *The Need for Roots*.

"Ripe as the melting cluster," *et al*. Handel and Gay.

"Arnica, eyebright, the / draft from the well with the / starred die above it, // in the / hut." Celan, "Todtnauberg."

Martin R.

"But the closeness of your being—and now your photographs—are so incontestable to me that, quite apart from knowing love, I will never believe you could or would live your life in 'idle experiments.'" Heidegger to Arendt, letter of 24 April 1925.

HAMLET: The body is with the king, but the king is not with the body. The king is a thing—
GUILDENSTERN: A thing, my lord!
HAMLET: Of nothing: bring me to him. Hide fox, and all after. (Hamlet 4.2)

"Polyphemus" *et al*. Handel and Gay.

Law of Ruin

"[T]he world, fabricated by men and constituted according to human and not natural laws, will become again part of nature, and will follow the law of ruin when man decides to become himself part of nature, a blind though accurate tool of natural laws, renouncing his supreme faculty of creating laws himself." Arendt, *Essays in Understanding*, quoted in Knott.

George Herbert "Love (3)"	Love bade me welcome. Yet my soul drew back

<pre>
                    Love bade me welcome. Yet my soul drew back
                              Guilty of dust and sin.
                    But quick-eyed Love, observing me grow slack
                              From my first entrance in,
                    Drew nearer to me, sweetly questioning,
                              If I lacked any thing.

                    A guest, I answered, worthy to be here:
                              Love said, You shall be he.
                    I the unkind, ungrateful? Ah my dear,
                              I cannot look on thee.
                    Love took my hand, and smiling did reply,
                              Who made the eyes but I?

                    Truth Lord, but I have marred them: let my shame
                              Go where it doth deserve.
                    And know you not, says Love, who bore the blame?
                              My dear, then I will serve.
                    You must sit down, says Love, and taste my meat:
                              So I did sit and eat.
</pre>

Interior Flesh

"Manual labor. Time entering into the body. Through work man turns himself into matter, as Christ does through the Eucharist. Work is like a death.

   "We have to pass through death. We have to be killed—to endure the weight of the world. When the universe is weighing upon the back of a human creature, what is there to be surprised at if it hurts him?

"Work is like a death if it is without an incentive. We have to act, renouncing the fruits of action.

"To work—if we are worn out it means that we are becoming submissive to time as matter is. Thought is forced to pass from one instant to the next without laying hold of the past or the future. That is what it means to obey." Weil, "The Mysticism of Work," *Gravity and Grace*.

"We have to cure our faults by attention and not by will.

"The will only controls a few movements of a few muscles, and these movements are associated with the idea of the change of position of near-by objects. I can will to put my hand flat on the table. If inner purity, inspiration or truth of thought were necessarily associated with attitudes of this kind, they might be the object of will. As this is not the case, we can only beg for them." Weil, "Attention and Will," *Gravity and Grace*.

"Where it is represented with such skill, intricate modulations affect the hideous truth. It becomes more graphic, more terribly defined, but also has more acceptable, conventional lodging in the imagination. We believe, yet we do not believe intolerably, for we draw breath at the recognition of a literary device, of a stylistic stroke not finally dissimilar from what we have met in a novel. The aesthetic makes endurable." Steiner, *op. cit.*

"It is called Love. I learned it by heart. Often, at the culminating point of a violent headache, I make myself say it over, concentrating all my attention upon it and clinging with all my soul to the tenderness it enshrines. I used to think I was merely reciting it as a beautiful poem, but without my knowing it the recitation had the virtue of a prayer." Weil, *Waiting on God*.

The Little Ice Age of Martin R.

"Indeed, the dying of others," *et al.* Heidegger, *Being and Time*.

The Human Artifice: Hannah R.

"In the case of art works, reification is more than mere transformation; it is transfiguration, a veritable metamorphosis in which it is as though the course of nature which wills that all fire burn to ashes is reverted and even dust can burst into flames. Works of art are thought things, but this does not prevent their being things." Arendt, *The Human Condition.*

Intense Inane

"Intense inane" is a phrase from English translations of Lucretius' *De Rerum Natura,* and adopted by P. B. Shelley for a speech in the penultimate act of his verse play *Prometheus Unbound:*

> The painted veil, by those who were, called life,
> Which mimicked, as with colors idly spread,
> All men believed and hoped, is torn aside;
> The loathsome mask has fallen, the man remains
> Sceptreless, free, uncircumscribed, but man
> Equal, unclassed, tribeless, and nationless,
> Exempt from awe, worship, degree, the king
> Over himself; just, gentle, wise; but man
> Passionless—no, yet free from guilt or pain,
> Which were, for his will made or suffered them;
> Nor yet exempt, though ruling them like slaves,
> From chance, and death, and mutability,
> The clogs of that which else might oversoar
> The loftiest star of unascended heaven,
> Pinnacled dim in the intense inane.

William Blake
Jerusalem

> Thus are the Heavens formed by Los within the Mundane Shell
> And where Luther ends Adam begins again in Eternal Circle
> To awake the Prisoners of Death; to bring Albion again
> With Luvah into light eternal, in his eternal day.

GAIAGONY / HANNAH FURIOSA

"The need of truth is more sacred than any other need. Yet it is never mentioned. One feels afraid to read when once one has realized the quantity and the monstrousness of the material falsehoods shamelessly paraded, even in the books of the most reputable authors. Thereafter one reads as though one were drinking from a contaminated well." Weil, *The Need for Roots.*

Celan   This
"Anabasis"   narrow sign between walls
                       the impassable-true
                       Upward and Back
                       to the heart-bright future.

Martin or Martin R.

Charles Olson   When the attentions change / the jungle
"The Kingfishers"   leaps in
                       even the stones are split
                                                 they rive

                       Or,
                       enter
                       that other conqueror we more naturally recognize
                       he so resembles ourselves

                       But the E
                       cut so rudely on that oldest stone
                       sounded otherwise,
                       was differently heard

"We want the creative faculty to imagine that which we know; we want the generous impulse to act that which we imagine; we want the poetry of life; our calculations have outrun conception; we have eaten more than we can digest." Shelley, "A Defence of Poetry"

Gigantic

Katastrophenhaft: the site of catastrophe: Heidegger's word for America. "The primacy of sheer quantity is itself a quality, i.e., an essential characteristic, which is that of boundlessness. This principle we call Americanism." Quoted in James W. Ceaser, *Reconstructing America.*

Heidegger "The Thinker as Poet"	All our heart's courage is the echoing response to the first call of Being which gathers our thinking into the play of the world. In thinking all things become solitary and slow. Patience nurtures magnanimity. He who thinks greatly must err greatly.
W.H. Auden "In Memory of W.B. Yeats"	With the farming of a verse Make a vineyard of the curse, Sing of human unsuccess In a rapture of distress

"A life spent entirely in public, in the presence of others, becomes, as we would say, shallow. While it retains its visibility, it loses the quality of rising into sight from some darker ground which must remain hidden if it is not to lose its depth in a very real non-subjective sense.

"The only efficient way to guarantee the darkness of what needs to be hidden against the light of publicity is private property, a privately owned place to hide in." Arendt, *The Human Condition*.

Thegonic Romcom of the Rising Seas

Minnie Riperton
"Loving You"
	Loving you
	    Is easy because you're beautiful
	    . . .
	No one else can make me feel
	The colors that you bring

"We understand already that Sisyphus is the hero of the absurd, as much because of his passions as from his torment. His contempt for the gods, his hatred of death, and his passion for life have earned him that indescribable torture in which his entire being strives to achieve nothing. Such is the price that must be paid for passion on this earth. We can say nothing of Sisyphus in hell; myths are made for the imagination to animate. For we see only the immense effort of a bent body to lift the enormous stone, to roll it and help it against gravity a hundred times over; we see the clenched face, cheek pressed against the stone, the shove of a shoulder receiving the clay-covered mass, a foot braced against it, the exhausted arms, the all-too-human security of two human hands filled with earth. At the end of this long effort measured by skyless space and depthless time, the goal is attained. Sisyphus then watches the stone drop in a few instants down to the world below, from which it will be necessary to once again climb toward the summits. He goes back down to the plain." Albert Camus, "The Myth of Sisyphus."

Gaiagony: Hannah and Martin

"The earth folded up here, folded once and twice and three times, and opened up in the middle, and in the middle there is water, and the water is green, and the green is white, and the white comes from even farther up, from the glaciers, and one could say, but one shouldn't, that this is the language that counts here, the green with the white in it, a language not for you and not for me—because, I ask you, for whom is it meant, the earth, not for you, I say, is it meant, and not for me—a language, well, without I and without You, nothing but He, nothing but It, you understand, and She, nothing but that." Celan, "Conversation in the Mountains."

"Everything seemed so small, so near, so wet, he would have liked to set the earth down behind an oven, he could not grasp why it took so much time to clamber down a slope, to reach a distant point; he was convinced he could cover it all with a pair of strides. . . . he would feel something tearing at his chest, he would stand there, gasping, body bent forward, eyes and mouth open wide, he was convinced he could draw the storm into himself, he stretched out and lay over the earth, he burrowed into the universe, it was a pleasure that gave him pain." Georg Büchner, *Lenz*.

"Can we perhaps now locate the strangeness, the place where the person was able to set himself free as an—estranged—I? Can we locate this place, this step?
   ". . . only, it sometimes bothered him that he could not walk on his head." This is Lenz. This is, I believe, his step, his 'Long live the king.'" Celan, "The Meridian."

"Yes, Reverend, you see, boredom! Boredom! O, sheer boredom, what more can I say, I have already drawn all the figures on the wall." Büchner, *Lenz*.

Letter to Olson as the Master [unsent]

This poem includes excerpts (italicized) from poems and commentary presented by Charles Olson at a series of lectures delivered at Goddard College in 1962. A transcript is available at the Slought Foundation: https://slought.org/media/files/olson_transcript.pdf

"Once upon a time there was a fox who was so lacking in slyness that he not only kept getting caught in traps but couldn't even tell the difference between a trap and a non-trap." Arendt, "Heidegger the Fox."

"If we want to know what absolute goodness would signify for the course of human affairs (as distinguished from the course of divine matters), we had better turn to the poets, and we can do it safely enough as long as we remember that 'the poet but embodies in verse those exaltations of sentiment that a nature like Nelson's, the opportunity being given, vitalizes into acts' (Melville). At least we can learn from them that absolute goodness is hardly any less dangerous than absolute evil, that it does not consist in selflessness, for surely the Grand Inquisitor is selfless enough, and that it is beyond virtue, even the virtue of Captain Vere. Neither Rousseau nor Robespierre was capable of dreaming of a goodness beyond virtue, just as they were unable to imagine that radical evil would 'partake nothing of the sordid or sensual' (Melville), that there could be wickedness beyond vice." Arendt, *On Revolution*.

Children of Saturn

Ezra Pound	The enormous tragedy of the dream in the peasant's bent
Pisan Cantos	shoulders
	Manes! Manes was tanned and stuffed,
	Thus Ben and la Clara *a Milano*
	by the heels at Milano
	That maggots shd/ eat the dead bullock
	Digonos, Διγονος, but the twice crucified
	where in history will you find it?

"We have to endure the discordance between imagination and fact.
    "It is better to say 'I am suffering' than 'this landscape is ugly.'" Weil, "Meaning of the Universe," *Gravity and Grace*.

The Works and Days of the Black Paintings

The poem includes, in italics, quotations from Hesiod, the "Ktaadn" passage from Henry David Thoreau's *The Maine Woods* ("What is this Titan that has possession of me?), the last lines of *King Lear,* and George Steiner's "A Kind of Survivor." The *Black Paintings* of Francisco Goya were originally painted as frescoes on the walls of the Quinta del Sordo (Deaf Man's House) occupied by Goya in the last years of his life. They are now on display at the Prada in Madrid.

Exterior Saints

"In any event, Augustine's observations on the impossibility of nilling absolutely because you cannot nill your own existence while you are nilling—hence cannot nill absolutely even by committing suicide—are an effective refutation of the mental tricks Stoic philosophers had recommended to enable men to withdraw from the world while still living in it." Arendt, *The Life of the Mind*.

"Augustine likens the way I recall what escapes my memory to the way I know, and possibly love or desire, what I am seeking. If it were altogether forgotten I would not recognize it. Indeed, I would not even know that I forgot something. This can easily be understood in the case of 'corporeal images,' where only an effort of the will is required to bring back to me the image of the city of Carthage that I saw before. However, 'it is indeed wondrous (*mirabile*) that the mind should see in itself what it saw nowhere else,' for example, 'what it means to be just.' In the same way we who seek the happy life and have no way of knowing what it is like know enough of its possible existence to seek and desire it. The way we know what the happy life is like is to know that it would be impossible if immortality were incompatible with human nature." Arendt, *Love and Saint Augustine*.

Kathryn Schulz, *op. cit*.

"Is it like the way we remember joy? Perhaps so, for even when I am sad, I remember joy, just as when I am miserable, I remember the happy life. But I never saw, or heard, or smelled, or tasted joy with a bodily sense. I experienced it in my mind when I rejoiced and knowledge of it has clung to my memory." Saint Augustine, *Confessions*.

"Hence, transcending the faculties of perception, which we have in common with the animals, and rising gradually to 'Him who made me,' Augustine arrives at 'the camps and vast palaces of memory.' There he finds the notion of the 'happy life,' which is his origin and as such the quintessence of his being. The absolute future turns out to be the ultimate past and the way to reach it is through remembrance." Arendt, *Love and Saint Augustine*.

"By destroying all space between men and pressing men against each other, even the productive potentialities of isolation are annihilated; by teaching and glorifying the logical reasoning of loneliness where man knows that he will be utterly lost if ever he lets go of the first premise from which the whole process is being started, even the slim chances that loneliness may be transformed into solitude and logic into thought are obliterated. If this practice is compared with that of tyranny, it seems as if a way had been found to set the desert itself in motion, to let loose a sand storm that could cover all parts of the inhabited earth." Arendt, *The Origins of Totalitarianism*.

Interior Medusa

"The Jew sticks like a bone in the throat of any other nationalism." Steiner, *op. cit.*

"Heisenberg showed conclusively that there is a definite and final limit to the accuracy of all measurements obtainable by man-devised instruments for those 'mysterious messengers from the real world.' The uncertainty principle "asserts that there are certain pairs of quantities, like the position and velocity of a particle, that are related in such a way that determining one of them with increased precision necessarily entails determining the other one with reduced precision. . . . From this he concluded that the modern search for 'true reality' behind mere appearances, which has brought about the world we live in and resulted in the Atomic Revolution, has led into a situation in the sciences themselves in which man has lost the very objectivity of the natural world, so that man in his hunt for "objective reality" suddenly discovered that he always 'confronts himself alone.'" Arendt, "The Conquest of Space."

Interior Birth

"That there be a beginning, man was created before whom there was nobody." Arendt's translation of Augustine's *Initium ergo ut esset, creatus est homo, ante quem nullus fuit, Love and Saint Augustine.*

Saint World

The poem includes a number of italicized lines taken from Simone Weil's "*The Iliad,* or the Poem of Force" and from *Gravity and Grace.*

"Ares is just, and kills those who kill"—Weil's version of lines from Book 18 of *The Iliad,* translated by William Cowper as "Mars his favors deals / Impartial, and the slayer oft is slain." The speech is made by Hector after slaying Patroclus and precedes his own humiliating death at the hands of Achilles.

Homer	. . . But Achilles
The Iliad	Wept, dreaming of the beloved comrade; sleep, all prevailing
	Would not take him; he turned over again and again.

"Even if it be against his harried will, his weariness, the Jew—or some Jews, at least—may have an exemplary role. To show that where trees have roots, men have legs and are each other's guests. If the potential of civilization is not to be destroyed, we shall have to develop more complex, more provisional loyalties. There are, as Socrates taught, necessary treasons to make the city freer and more open to man." Steiner, *op. cit.*

Celan	Visible, audible thing, the
"Anabasis"	tent-
	word growing free:
	Together.

"Between two people, sometimes, how rarely, a world grows. It is then one's homeland; in any case, it was the only homeland we were willing to recognize. This tiny microworld where you can always escape from the world, and which disintegrates when the other has gone away. . . . I go now and am quite calm and think: away." Letter from Arendt to Heidegger after the death of her husband Heinrich Blücher.

Gaiagony

"*Know that I am hiding something from you,* that is the active paradox I must resolve: *at one and the same time* it must be known and not known: know that I don't want to show it: that is the message I address to the other. *Larvatus prodeo:* I advance pointing to my mask: I put a mask on my passion, but with a discreet (and wily) finger I designate this mask." Roland Barthes, *Roland Barthes by Roland Barthes*.

"Absolutely unmixed attention is prayer." Weil, "Attention and Will," *Gravity and Grace*.

"Justice and love, which have hardly any place in this study of extremes and of unjust acts of violence, nevertheless bathe the work in their light without ever becoming noticeable themselves, except as a kind of accent. Nothing precious is scorned, whether or not death is its destiny; everyone's unhappiness is laid bare without dissimulation or disdain; no man is set above or below the condition common to all men; whatever is destroyed is regretted." Weil, "*The Iliad,* or the Poem of Force."

"If the propaganda of truth fails to convince the average person because it is too monstrous, it is positively dangerous to those who know from their own imaginings what they themselves are capable of doing and who are therefore perfectly willing to believe in the reality of what they have seen." Arendt, *The Origins of Totalitarianism*.

"Efforts of those who, with man-made stars flying overhead, unsheltered even by the traditional tent of the sky, exposed in an unsuspected, terrifying way, carry their existence into language, racked by reality and in search of it." Celan, "Bremen Speech."

"What, if some day or night a demon were to steal after you into your loneliest loneliness and say to you: 'This life as you now live it and have lived it, you will have to live once more and innumerable times more' . . . Would you not throw yourself down and gnash your teeth and curse the demon who spoke thus? Or have you once experienced a tremendous moment when you would have answered him: 'You are a god and never have I heard anything more godly.'" Friedrich Nietzsche, *The Gay Science*.

"He who does not realize to what extent shifting fortune and necessity hold in subjection every human spirit, cannot recognize as fellow-creatures nor love as he loves himself those whom chance separated from him by an abyss. The variety of constraints pressing upon man give rise to the illusion of several distinct species that cannot communicate. Only he who has measured the dominion of force, and knows how to respect it, is capable of love and justice." Weil, "*The Iliad,* or the Poem of Force."

"Let the whole universe be for me, in relation to my body, what the stick of a blind man is in relation to his hand. His sensibility is really no longer in his hand but at the end of the stick. An apprenticeship is necessary.

"To limit one's love to the pure object is the same thing as to extend it to the whole universe. . . .

"May this object be the universe, the seasons, the sun, the stars." Weil, "Meaning of the Universe," *Gravity and Grace.*

"And *who* are we? . . . the fact that attempts to define the nature of man lead so easily into an idea which definitely strikes us as 'superhuman' and therefore is identified with the divine may cast a suspicion upon the very concept of human nature. On the other hand, the conditions of human existence—life itself, natality and mortality, worldliness, plurality, and the earth—can never 'explain' what we are or answer the question of who we are for the simple reason that they never condition us absolutely." Arendt, *The Human Condition.*

"When poetry . . ."

"The *accusative* of violence, like that of love, destroys the in-between, crushes or burns it, renders the other defenseless, strips itself of protection. [The other becomes the *über,* the "about," the object.] In contrast to this stands the *dative* of saying and speaking, which confirms the in-between, moves within it [the *mit,* the "with," the given]. Then again there is the accusative of the singing poem, which removes and releases what it sings from [the *from*] the in-between and its relations, without confirming anything. When poetry and not philosophy absolutizes, there's rescue." Arendt, *Denktagebuch,* August 1953.

ACKNOWLEDGMENTS

The spirit of twentieth-century European Jewish aesthetico-political thought illuminates and endarkens this text: Arendt, Benjamin, and Celan are its ABC, Simone Weil its apostate saint. But there are many other characters.

Thanks to the following poets, readers, and friends without whom this book would not have found its form: Norman Finkelstein, Michael Heller, Robert Archambeau, and Sandra Simonds offered valuable feedback, fellowship, endorsement, and support. A special thank you to the late Benjamin Hollander, whose enthusiasm and encouragement came at a crucial time. You are much missed.

Thank you to Janet Holmes for her steadfast support of this project, and for her brilliant work as editor, publisher, and designer. American poetry is the richer for your work.

Thank you to Marc Vincenz and MadHat Press for rescuing this work from limbo and for their editorial curation and care.

Thanks to the following editors and journals for publishing portions of this work while it was still in progress: Shira Dentz, *Tarpaulin Sky;* Benjamin Hollander, *Letters for Olson;* Paul Hoover, *New American Writing;* Andrew Wessels and Ryan Winet, *The Offending Adam*; and Kirstin Hotelling Zona, *Spoon River Poetry Review.*

I dedicate this book to the memory of my mother and father. To my daughter, who must live in the world we're making. And to Emily, steadfast and true.

ABOUT THE AUTHOR

JOSHUA COREY is a poet, novelist, translator, and critic. His other books include the poetry collections *Severance Songs* and *The Barons*; a collection of critical prose, *The Transcendental Circuit: Otherworlds of Poetry*; a new translation, with Jean-Luc Garneau, of Francis Ponge's first book of prose poems as *Partisan of Things*; and a novel, *Beautiful Soul: An American Elegy*. With G.C. Waldrep he co-edited *The Arcadia Project: North American Postmodern Pastoral* (Ahsahta Press, 2012). He lives in Evanston, Illinois and teaches English at Lake Forest College.

www.ingramcontent.com/pod-product-compliance
Lightning Source LLC
Chambersburg PA
CBHW042023180426
43199CB00039B/2927